THE BOY
Who Never Lived

by

Frederick MSK Mak-Poole

Grosvenor House
Publishing Limited

This book is published by
Grosvenor House Publishing Ltd
Link House
140 The Broadway, Tolworth, Surrey, KT6 7HT.
www.grosvenorhousepublishing.co.uk

This book is a work of fiction. Any resemblance to
people or events, past or present, is purely coincidental.

A CIP record for this book
is available from the British Library

ISBN 978-1-78623-222-9

This is my first book and it has been professionally proofed and edited.

It is all my own work.

As you will read the profits from this book are to form the cornerstone that will be

The MSK. Foundation.

Contents

Preface

Life on this earth is not easy, many things can go wrong, and we can and do inflict terrible pain upon each other, whether that be knowingly or in some cases unknowingly, or through just being insensitive, reckless, or callous, and even infectious acts of abuse and rape.

We can carry our pain around with us for many years and in extreme cases whole lifetimes; I carried my pain for thirty-five years. As a young boy I was very angry and expelled from school at the age of 15 years old, illiterate and broken, branded as thick, lazy, and stupid, and frequently slapped around the ear just to re-enforce it. As a young man, I was very confused, bitter and twisted.

This is a book of fiction based on facts that you may not believe to be true, it is up to you the reader to decide what you want to believe. The presentation is inspired by actual events, the characters are composite or fictionalized and incidents are fictionalized or created for dramatic purpose. All the actual names and locations have been changed.

How is it that so many people must suffer at the hands of others? What is it about humanity that so many people think that the abuse and rape of children is ok if they can get away with it? And what of the damage and devastation of the lives of their victims?

This book is a life story that starts in post war England in 1954. The reason for the book is to assist in laying the cornerstone for the MSK foundation. This started as a vision in the summer of 2004, now it will soon to be a reality.

This book will take you on a rollercoaster ride of emotions, it starts with the struggle of a boy at the tender age of ten, when his father died suddenly, then the grooming by a local vicar and his friend that leads to six years of abuse and rape on an almost daily basis, the boy's struggle at school and being branded as being, thick, lazy and stupid, and the constant clips around the ears to re-enforce it. The sense and feeling that he was in some way complicit with the acts and the impregnation with a spiritual beast that fed on the boy's pain and suffering.

As a young man serving many years in the armed forces and his time as a police officer, looking for answers to his confusion and pain, the many train wrecks in his life, then eventually serving eight years in some of the UK's worst Victorian prisons.

A massive white light in the darkness and his need to grasp that light, the constant battle ground between the darkness and the light, the eventual destruction of the beast and the new re-born man, full of hope and put right with himself, now in the true story he was always meant to be in.

Acknowledgments

LaiLeng Mak-Poole, my amazing wife. Without her this book would not be possible. Rev Tim Mayfield. Formally a minister at St Mark's Church, Battersea Rise, London; Georgie Pearson-Gee, St Mark's Church, Battersea Rise, London; Di Baily, St Mark's Church, Battersea Rise, London; Sarah Spreckley, St Mark's Church, Battersea Rise, London.

About the Author

As a young boy he was battered and bruised, abused and raped, he was impregnated without knowing it, with a spiritual beast, that fed off his agony, anger and pain, like a leach trying to draw every drop of blood it can. He was confused and had lost his identity, lost his sexuality and purpose, was on the edge of humanity looking in, a loner, never fitting in. he served in the armed forces and was a police officer, always struggling and making bad or wrong decisions in his life. He became an expert at hiding and manipulation of recovery and dusting himself down, a fighter and survivor, but never fitting in, always on the outside looking in. he would bounce from one relationship to the next, one job to the next, never staying in one place too long, always burning his bridges behind him, he couldn't relate to people, was often suspicious, totally paranoid and looking for an angle.

He would talk about love a lot, he would even crave for love, but when it was genuinely offered to him he could not engage with it or recognize it for what it was, and he destroyed it for being false and ill-intended such was his confusion and the power of the beast, his best friend was the devil who controlled the beast, he understood the beast and liked its golden rule; hurt them before they hurt you again.

He never understood sadness but was an expert in pain; he never knew compassion because he was an expert at indifference and heartlessness, He was totally in the wrong story, not the one that was intended for his life.

CHAPTER ONE

Freddie's Birthday

The time 14.22 on Saturday 8 September 1954, I am still in my bubble inside my mum's belly, on the outside yet to be known to me are four sisters and four brothers, I don't know their names as we have yet to be introduced, well I think it's about time for me to show myself, better give mum a big kick. It's a bit of a struggle I am nearly there – POP – out I come, the very first thing I hear is my Dad, "Well done Lily, (that's my mum) it's a healthy little boy, ten fingers and ten toes".

"Yes, and it will be the last one," Mum screams at my Dad!

Mum and dad had been out for a walk in the park near where we lived, Stanley Park in the centre of Liverpool, right in the middle of two great football teams, Liverpool FC and Everton FC the greater being Liverpool of course. Well mum delivered me in the groundsmen's shed in the park and after a short stay in Stanley Road Hospital, mum and I are taken home, 37, Pugin Street, right near to Anfield football stadium, the home of Liverpool Football Club.

Our house is an old pre-war terraced house two up and two down, the front door is right on the street, as you go through the front door on the left is the front downstairs room, with a coal fire and a double put-me-up bed and my pram, then the back room is the kitchen leading through the back door to the yard. In the yard is the outside loo, and the mangle for draining and ringing the washing and hanging on the wall is a big steel bath, we only had cold water, if mum wanted hot

1

water it had to be boiled up on the cooker. From the back door, stairs to go upstairs to just two rooms one in the front, with a double bed in it and a wardrobe and in the back room the same; the front room was for the four boys and the back room for the four girls.

1962 – Spring time. I am now eight years old.

For the most part life was good, even though mum and dad struggled to put food on the table and a shirt on my back, post war northern England was hard going with eleven mouths to feed, we didn't know any different it was just the way life was in those days. As soon as the sun came up our chores had to be done, mum had everyone working like clockwork, once our chores were done then that was the lot of us out in the street regardless of the weather, mum had three jobs every day seven days a week. Dad could not work due to his injuries from the war, I didn't know what the injuries were as no one would speak to me about it.

I really loved my dad, I was definitely his boy, he would take me everywhere with him as I was growing up, he would play snooker at the local working men's club, and was in fact the local snooker league referee. On Sundays he would take me to the club with him, I knew all the guys in the club because of my dad, he was very famous and everyone knew him, he was a great big man 6ft 8in, he had to bend his head to get through the door, the funny thing was that my mum was only 4ft 8ins. When I asked dad about that he just laughed and said, "don't worry Freddie we are all the same lying down, and you don't have to worry, you will grow up to be big and strong just like me.

Walking along the road, I would have to really reach up to hold my dad's hand, I used to think he was a real live giant, as we walked together everyone knew my dad, "Hello Sam," they would shout (that's my dad's name), "How ye doing little Freddie?" (that's me).

Dad would reply, "Very well thank you!" and I would say, "We are going to the club!"

When we got to the club, I would sit in the corner of the snooker hall, a special table that would always be kept for my dad, Steve the club barman said to me, "The usual Freddie"? and I would answer him, "Yes please Steve".

My dad always had the same a pint of mild and bitter, I would always have a glass of lemonade and a bag of crisps with a little blue rap of salt in the bottom, "Make that last our Freddie" my dad would say, but Steve would always bring me a top up when my dad wasn't looking.

Dad had his routine, he would walk around the table looking at it from every angle, then he would take a ball and role it in different directions across the table to make sure it was level, then when he was happy he would go to the rack on the wall and take his cue down. He had his own special cue and no one was allowed to use it, Dad would hand it to me and I would take it out of the case, in the case was a special cloth and Dad's own chalk, I would give Dad his chalk and he would put it in the pocket of his waistcoat. I would give the cue a good polish with the cloth, I would then stand at the end of the table until dad was ready, then when dad was ready he would give a bellow, "Who would like a lesson then? Come along don't be shy".

There would always be people queuing up to take Dad on, this day after Dad had won about five games, Dad's friend, Chutney Chas, stepped up, "Ok Sam (my dad) its time you learnt how to lose".

"That will be the day," Dad replied with a cheeky smile on his face, it was a close game but again my dad won. The game was intense and it was played in complete silence, if anyone made the slightest sound they would get a very stern look from my dad, and a look was all that was needed. It was great to watch my dad in action, when all the challenges where over it would be time to go home, "Let's go Freddie, Mum will have our dinner ready".

I would pack dads cue away after I had given it a polish, Dad would give me his chalk to put back in the case and then he would put it back in its place on the wall, we would say our goodbyes and be on our way. My dad was great and we got home just as Mum was putting the dinner on the table, "Wash ye hands mum would say".

Everyone would be around the table, the table was two trestles my dad had made and then the top was a big piece of wood dad had got from the mill, we all had our own stools, and dad made them all, mum said as each one of us was born dad would make a stool and put our names on the underneath, Sunday was the only day in the week we would have meat – nearly always chicken – after dinner everyone had their chores to do, the table would be cleared away, dad would have a nap, and mum would do her sewing and knitting with the girls. In the summer me and my brothers would be allowed out to play footy in the street, there were no cars in those; days nobody in our street could afford one.

This Sunday as we were let out to play some of the kids were waiting for me, Kermit shouted to me, "Henry has called you out, he is on the rec and you had better take ye brothers, I think there's going to be blood".

I shouted back with great confidence, "I don't need my brothers for Henry!" I was trembling, the rec was at the end of the street, it was one of the bombed-out houses, and all the rubble had been cleared, Henry was the biggest kid in the street, but if I had told my brothers I would be in trouble with my dad because he always said we had to fight our own battles. Off to the wreck I went with all the kids following me, shouting, "Fight, fight, fight" when I got to the wreck Henry was there with the rest of the kids from the street, he started calling me a grass, he was taller than me and a year older, but if you are called out, ye called out. So there we were toe to toe, Henry calling me a grass, then Henry made the first move and as he went to push me I stepped to my right, jumped up and

4

landed him a right on the side of the head, I remember all the shaking just stopping instantly my punch landed, all the kids where shouting and the fight was on. Henry got a good few punches in, and by the time Henry had declared "Arley-barley" that means he gave up, he had two black eyes and what looked like a broken nose and I had one black eye and a cut lip, but because he gave up first, by declaring "Arley-barley" it meant I had won the fight.

Henry had got into trouble off his dad for stealing sweets from the paper shop, and assumed that I had grassed him up because his dad was told by someone at the snooker club, so because I am the only kid in the street that was allowed in the club, he thought it was me. Anyway as I walked up the street back to my house all my brothers and sisters were in the street and as I walked up to them, my big brother Barney, give me a dig and shouted at me to go and finish him off, I shouted at Barney, "Go and look at him, he is still on the deck, I won".

Barney started chasing me around my brothers and sisters and shortly after we were all called in by my big sister Abbey. When we went in Mum said let me have a look at that eye and put a cold wet cloth on it.

Dad shouted, "Well did ye win our Freddie".

"Yes Dad," I replied.

"Good," he said, "got to stand up for ye-self in this world. Right you lot get ye-selves ready for bed, now, school tomorrow."

What Henry didn't know was I was more scared of my brothers and my dad than I was of him, so really, he never stood a chance.

It was a good thing I gave Henry a good beating, goodness knows what Dad would have done, and my brothers would have been in trouble for not looking out for me. It took a while for my black eye and my bruising to go down, but I was happy because Henry had two black eyes' and all that week no one had to ask who had won the fight. Afterwards Henry always tried to keep on my good side, little did he know that I didn't have a bad side, I just had no choice other than to knock his block off. I seemed to get a lot of respect in our street after all that, respect my dad said I had deserved and I had earned all for myself. Before the fight with Henry I used to get respect but it was because of my dad and family, Dad said it was a good thing I could look after myself as it was a tough old world.

* * *

The summertime was great as we could all go up the road to Stanley Park, it was mum's favourite place and it was just at the top of our street, it was where I was born. There was a great big tree in the park, right next to one of the fences, the tree was called lofty because it was so big, one of the main branches ran along the side of the park fence, the fence was really tall a lot bigger than me, and the big kids, like all my brothers, would play a game. The game was called lofty – after the tree – my brothers and other kids would climb up to the first big branch that was higher than the fence, then one by one they would jump off the tree over the fence and land on the pavement by the road, my job was to mark were they each landed with a piece of stone.

One day, after it had been raining, all the gang from our street were up the park playing lofty, it was my brother Zak's turn to jump. Just as he jumped his foot slipped and he fell upside down onto the top of the fence, the fence was made of metal and on the top was big speared heads, the spear head went right in the back of Zak's leg and then out the front and he was hanging upside down, he was squealing like a pig. I know what that's like because now and then mum sent us up the end of the park where the slaughter house was to get some pig's trotters, just as they came off the pigs. They made great broth and soup, my mum was really clever like that.

Right, back to the story, so some men came over and got Zak off the fence, all my sisters had heard the commotion and ran over to lofty, a great crowd of people had gathered and my sister Rosa grabbed my hand and started with me home.

"Rosa, Rosa," I shouted as I dug my heels in to stop Rosa dragging me off, "I need to get you home there will be murder when dad finds out!"

As we turned into our road my big sis Pat (short for Patricia) had already gone ahead and got mum, and they were both hurrying up our street, as we pasted them mum shouted to Rosa, "keep Freddie at home and if ye da comes home say nothing."

I tried to say to mum, "But mum," that was as far as I got. Rosa had a firm grip on my hand, and I was still digging my heels in as much as I could, we got to the house and Rosa said, "Go upstairs Freddie and be a good boy".

I went upstairs to the front room looking out of the window, after a short while I saw my dad marching down the street, he did not look happy as he bounced in the front door. Rosa in her best happy voice said, "Ye want a cupper dad".

"Don't try and be sweet," he growled at Rosa, "make me tea then get up to that hospital and tell ye ma to get home now".

I was peeking through the stair railings, Rosa looked at dad shocked.

"Yes, I know all about it," Dad said to Rosa.

I thought my dad must be a magic man?

"Get on with ye girl and tell our Freddie to get off the stairs and get down here".

As Rosa ran out the door she shouted, "Freddie get down here to ye da".

I composed myself and with a cheeky smile I walked into the front room. Dad was having his cup of tea.

"Hey Dad," I said.

"Ok Son, sit on that stool and tell me all," he had a very stern look on his face. Well I wasn't going to risk anything with my dad, and I know that you shouldn't grass on people, but this was my dad and I was within striking distance and nowhere to run, so I spilled the beans on all I knew.

* * *

A while later everyone was back from the hospital even our Zak, he was carried in and taken upstairs all his leg was bandaged from top to bottom.

"Freddie get ye self of to bed," Dad said to me. It wasn't yet bedtime for me but it was one of those times ye didn't argue, off I went and I wasn't half way up the stairs and I could hear dad start on my brothers and sisters, as he had them all lined up in the front room.

"Well that will teach him a lesson," Dad started "and I have seen worse in the war," he continued.

I could hear Mum already sobbing in the back kitchen, "Stop that wailing women," Dad shouted, then I heard the back door go and Mum continued her sobbing in the back yard, I felt so sad for my mum, and as Dad got on with my brothers and sisters with his belt I got under the bed covers and was crying, but as quiet as I could. Our Zak was next to me and I could see he was in a lot of pain and we just hung on to each other under the covers, the noise seemed to go on for ages and one by one as my brothers and sisters came upstairs crying, as Dad finished with them, I thought that night was never going to end.

The next morning we all got up as if nothing had happened, except Zak, who could only walk with the big wooden crutches he had been given by the hospital, he scooted down the stairs on his bum – it looked funny – Dad wouldn't let anyone help him.

He said, "You got yourself into that mess you can just get on with it".

Well it wasn't long before everything was back to normal, Zak's leg was ok apart from some cracking big scars, he already had a war story to go with the scars.

* * *

Dad was often unwell due to the war, my mum said, one time he was very bad, and I got sent to my aunty Floe's house, that's my mum's sister, aunty Floe and uncle Fred; he was named after me! I would normally go to Floe's house when anything serious was going on, but I didn't mind because aunty Floe and uncle Fred never had any kids of their own and they had a big house, just on the edge of the city, everyone said that they were posh, really they were just aunty Floe and uncle Fred that lived in the big house, Floe was great and she would spoil me all the time, Fred was magic, he could make anything, especially radios, he had a big mast in the back garden – that was one of the ways you could tell that they were posh – because they had a garden, anyway Fred often would listen to the police radios, and he got into trouble very often, he was called a radio ham! One time he even got taken to the police station in handcuffs, and all his equipment got taken away, Fred used to be an important radio man in the war, and every time they took his equipment the next day he would go and get more.

After my stay was over, Floe took me back home on the bus, when we got there Dad was in hospital and everyone was putting everything into bags and sacs, and some big old crates had been packed.

"What is happening?" I asked.

"We are being moved," mum said.

"Where are we going?"

My big sister Fern (she is the oldest) said, "It will be ok Freddie, we are going to a big house and very shortly a truck is coming to pick us all up and take all our things to the new house, it's posh like aunty Floe's and has a big garden in the front and the back, and it will be great".

CHAPTER TWO

The New House – 1959

We all got into a big army truck, I remember thinking that all we had as a family apart from dad was now in this truck, what if we wasn't going to a new house and really the Jerries had won the war and we was going off to a prisoner of war camp. I got quite nervous and started to think all sorts of things about what a prison camp would be like. I had been told lots of stories, what if they were true?

Nervously I said to my brother Adam, "Are we really going to a new house?"

"Yes Freddie," he answered.

"It won't take long," said my sister Megan, as she put her arm around me, we were sat on one of the mattresses,

"It is just outside the city, a new town," Zak shouted to me from the other end of the truck, and then before I knew it we were there, everyone got out of the truck.

I was amazed. "Is this all ours?" I shouted out as I ran into the front garden, Mum soon stopped us in our tracks, "get everything off the truck before you all go in the house and put it all on the grass".

That was our new front garden, it had proper grass – just like at Stanley Park – everyone was so excited including my mum, when we got everything of the truck the driver went, and right across the other side of the road was a great big field, bigger than Stanley Park. I think I was in shock.

There was a man and a women on the step with the front door open, the lady said, "Hello Mrs Taylor, welcome to your new home," and gave mum a bunch of keys. Mum said we could all go in and look around, I went right through the hall into a massive kitchen, then as I looked through the window I could see a great big garden out the back,

Zak opened the back door and we went out, there was a big coal shed you could sleep in, then another big brick shed we could all sleep in, and the garden was massive, everyone was so excited. We had the hall, a downstairs toilet, a big room in the front, a big room in the back, a big kitchen, then up the stairs was a landing that was as big as our old room, a bedroom then the bathroom, with a toilet and a sink, hot and cold water, then another three big bedrooms, Megan pulled down on a rope tied to the wall and a hatch and magic stairs came down from the roof, we went up and there was a great big loft; the whole house was amazing.

I asked mum, "When will Dad be home to see the new house?"

"The day after tomorrow, all being well," she replied.

I was so excited, whatever will Dad think? Everyone was claiming their rooms and beds, no more head to toe, I don't know how we all got to sleep that night and we would have been happy with the shed!

* * *

It wasn't long before Dad was home, but it seemed to be so different, there was an edge about everything, Mum and all my brothers and sisters seemed to be less happy and even on edge, I just could not understand it.

Well, as the days and weeks went by I thought we were really posh, we had a living room and what my mum called the *parla*, although mum could not use it as a *parla*, whatever that was, because a bed had been put up in that room because Dad could not walk up the stairs, it seemed that as Dad got more and more ill his belt came out more and more, mum seemed to be upset a lot and no one would talk about Dad or even give him a mention, I spent a lot of time with Dad in that room, it seemed as if no one else wanted to.

Well by now it was just getting to the start of the summer and all the talk with my brothers and sisters was about which farm they would go to for the picking. My brother Bruce said they should go to Rhymers Farm, because now that we had moved out of the city, we were closer to that farm and it would only take us an hour to get there. Everyone agreed, my brothers and sisters would go picking on the farms every year, it was good work they said, and would help Mum put food on the table. I had never gone with them as Mum said I was to small and it was a long way to walk, well this year it was closer and I pestered everyone to let me go with them, they could be picking spuds, lettuce, beans, sprouts later in the year and all sorts of things, they would come back with lots of tales of what happened, and I always wanted to go with them. This year Mum finally said to me, "If it is ok with ye dad you can go".

I was right into Dad's room and in a very soft vice I said, "Dad can I go spud picking tomorrow?"

Dad looked really white, almost like a ghost, and for a moment I thought he was dead, then all of a sudden he looked at me and said, "What is it my little one?" with a smile on his face.

I thought that's it I am in now, "Dad," I said, "can I go picking tomorrow?"

"So long as you bring me some nice fresh beans," Dad said. I was out the door and into the kitchen to speak to Mum before anyone could change their minds.

"Yes Mum, I can go, Dad said I could".

"Ok," Mum said, "you had better get to bed early because everyone will be leaving at five am".

"Great I can go," I told every one of my brothers and sisters about ten times each, I don't think I was too existed, do you?

* * *

Five am the next morning

I don't know how long I had been up and ready, I think everyone was ready now.

"Mum has left some food wrapped up in the larder," I said to my sisters.

"Yes we know," came a reply.

Mum was up and sitting on the front step, as I sat beside her.

"Good morning," she said as I sat beside her.

"They won't go without me mum will they?"

"No son," mum replied

Then all of a sudden Zack said in a firm voice, "everyone ready? Let's go"

I need to say goodbye to Dad," and I got up.

Then Mum grabbed my arm, "No Son" she said, "Dad is still asleep and the Doctor is coming out to see Dad this morning so let him sleep".

"Ok mum," and we all started down the garden path towards an iron gate at the end, we actually had a path I can't believe it, off across the field we went with the girls saying, "You are going the wrong way" and pointing up our street.

"This is a short cut," Zack said and waved his arm so they would follow, and they did, "At the end of the field we just cut across the railway line then we will be on the road that leads all the way to the farm," Zack said.

Megan said, "How do you know that?"

"I did a recce yesterday," he replied.

* * *

Before we knew it, we were at the farm, a big man was in the farmyard and holding his arms out with a big smile he shouted, "Here they are my number one team, just in time and looks like they have a recruit".

"Hi Mr Rhymer"

My brother shouted back, "This is our youngest brother Freddie his first time picking".

"That's great," said farmer Rhymer, "ok let's get you all sorted out, You will be picking beans this morning and potatoes this afternoon, you will all have to show little Freddie the ropes".

"Not a problem, we will all look after him," my brother said.

As we got to the field with the beans in my sister Megan gave me a basket and said, "You will have to be careful of the stinging nettles," they were as big as the beans and all bigger than me. "You see the stinging nettles Freddie, before we finish we will get a big bag of the young ones to take home to mum".

"Why?" I asked, and she said that mum would love them to make nettle soup and to dry some of the leaves to keep for nettle tea.

***

It was a long hard day and at the end of the day brother Zack was getting paid for us all by the farmer Mr Rhymer.

The farmer said, "Now little Freddie you did very well for your first day and I want you to give these fresh field mushrooms to your mum, as a thank you from me for letting you come today".

"Wow thanks, mum will be so happy, thanks."

On our way home we had a cart full of beans, potatoes, carrots and turnips, we had picked some and some we had paid for out of our wages, "Mum will be so pleased," Adam said as he lifted me up onto the cart so I could get a ride home and we could get home quicker.

We arrived home and we could see Mum sitting on the front doorstep, I jumped off the cart and started waving and shouting, but she didn't wave back at all.

"Do you think she can see us?" I asked.

"Yes she can see us, but something is wrong".

What can it be I thought, I looked at all my brothers and sisters and you would think they had seen a ghost, I started to run towards Mum waving, and Zack grabbed hold of me, "hold on Freddie," he said, "let's find out what is wrong first".

As we got closer mum got up off the step and went in the house, as we got to the gate mum shouted, "Freddie you get in here," Mum was in the kitchen, "the rest of you take the cart out the back and sort it all out in the shed, then you need to all go upstairs".

My middle sister Rosa came in with me as we got to the kitchen Rosa said, "what is it Mum?" grabbing hold of my hand as if her life depended on it.

"Never you mind Rosa, go and stay upstairs, ye dad wants to speak with Freddie."

In the past that usually meant that someone was going to get dad's belt, it couldn't be for me I was Dad's favourite, and I hadn't done anything wrong, just then Dad game out of his room with his belt in his hand.

"There you are my lad, tell lies to your mother would you?"

"I don't know what you are talking about Dad," as I started to tremble.

"Get in here," he said.

"But Mum what is Dad talking about?" I cried out.

"Your dad didn't say you could go picking did he?"

"Yes mum, yes Dad," I cried out, with a blink of an eye dad had hold of me by the scruff of my shirt, dragged me into his room and put me over the back of the chair, as the first lash came across my backside dad shouted, "this will teach you to tell lies".

I put my hand in my mouth and bit down on it so I could not scream, then another lash and another.

"Six of the best for you my lad," then as Dad pulled me up he looked right at me and said, "No tears Freddie, that's good it will make a man of you".

My backside was on fire and as I came out of Dad's room, Mum put her finger in front of her mouth as to say don't speak a word and then pointed to the stairs, as I got to the top of the stirs, my sisters where all in the bedroom waiting with cold wet towels, they stripped my pants off me, put me on the bed face down and then covered me with the towels, at first they stung, but then it started to take away the pain. Dad had never whipped me like that before and as I started to recover from the pain I said to my sisters, "I never told a lie honest I didn't".

My sister Patricia had my pyjamas ready and said quietly, "You had better get into bed now and sleep it off, I will bring you some supper later".

I was in so much in pain I fell asleep on my belly, the next morning mum got me up and said, "Now Freddie when you come down not a word about yesterday".

"Ok mum," I said.

When I went downstairs, it was about 8am and mum had some bread and dripping for me, all my brothers and sisters had already gone to the farm picking. I never did know why dad gave me the lashes with the belt and I wasn't allowed to go picking ever again, the strange thing was no one ever spoke about it, it was as if it had never happened, well I knew it happened I had to sit on a cushion for a week.

* * *

Sometime later my dad, mum and I had been working on the gardens, they started to look good, Mum said Dad had green fingers because he was so good, and he started to get better, the front gardens were a small lawn around rose beds and all sorts of flowers around the edges, the back garden was some lawn and mostly a vegetable section for runner beans, carrots, turnips and potatoes. Dad said I didn't need to go to the farms picking, I had my own.

That summer was so good, but towards the end of it dad became ill again and his bed was put back in the downstairs front room. Dad had been in hospital again and was now home, he seemed very grey and I had to ask Mum if I wanted to go in his room to see him. I was allowed sometimes and

Dad and me would talk about when he used to play snooker and how good the garden was looking.

"You did very good Freddie," he said, he was speaking about how I had helped in the garden, I never mentioned about going picking at the farm ever again.

Dad seemed to be getting worse and I could not see him for a whole week, then Mum packed me off to aunty Floe's again, I was there for about two weeks and when I came home Dad's bed had been moved upstairs.

I said to Mum, "Is dad well now mum?"

Mum and Floe took me in the front room, it had all been done up posh, I sat down on the chair and Mum got hold of both of my hands, "I have something very important to tell you," she said with a very straight face, as she said it aunty Floe was on the arm of the chair next to me, she put her arm around me and started to squeeze me, I thought heck what is coming now?

Floe said, "It will all be ok Freddie"

What will, I thought as my heart started to come up into my mouth, and Mum and aunty Floes grip on me got tighter, "Your dad has died Freddie," Mum said,

"Is he coming home?" I asked.

"No," Floe answered, "he has gone to heaven".

"More like hell," Mum snarled, I never knew where heaven was, or hell.

"Can I go there and see him?"

"No," mum said "he has died and you won't be seeing him anymore".

I got so upset as the information started to sink in with some more prompting from Floe and mum, then I started screaming and shouting, Mum shouted for my sisters to come and help her, I was carted upstairs and literally sat on till I started to calm down and it eventually sunk in that I would not see dad again.

Dad was never mentioned in the family ever again, if I tried to mention anything about dad, I would be shut up and the subject instantly changed, it was to be 41 years later that I would even find out where dad was buried.

***

July 2015.

Sefton Park Cemetery, plot 5279, marked by a lump of concrete six inches long, four inches wide and two inches thick, in the ground with Dad's grave number on it, 5279, no name no recognition of who is buried there, no flowers, less fuss than you would give to a pet cat or dog. What could it be that dad had done so wrong that he was just forgotten? He had served in the Royal Navy in the Second world War, his ship was sunk in the Atlantic Ocean, he was a war veteran with four medals, acknowledged by the Queen and country, but never acknowledged by his family as ever being alive!

Then there is me, what have I been up to for 41 years? Well this might come as a shock to you but I have just come out of prison after serving eight years, no parole, time served, in some of the UK's worst Victorian prisons, I can see the shock on your faces, the only thing I promised myself was I would find out what had happened to my dad! So why don't I take you back now to 1964.

CHAPTER THREE

Liverpool – 1964

Liverpool, we are still in our new house, things are ok, no one at all talking about my dad. Mum is doing extra work for the local church, cleaning the church in the week, cleaning for the vicar, and doing his laundry. I am in school now, I never had to go when my Dad was alive, he used to say he would teach me all I needed to know about the world, now I am in school I get picked on a bit, because the teacher calls me thick and lazy. I can't read and write like all the other kids, and they only pick on me from a distance because they all know that they would get a good right hook if they got too close. It is a big school and lots of places to hide, some of the kids bunk off, but I can't do that, my mum would kill me, so I have got very good at hiding.

Some days my mum would meet me from school and take me with her to clean the church, it was good fun and I got time with my mum on her own, and the church was huge, mum would do different parts on different days, one time I was cleaning all the seats with a duster and I heard this voice behind me from a distance, "So this is little Freddie then".

I crapped myself, I thought it was God talking to me, and I ducked down behind the seat, as I peered over the back of the seat, I saw mum and a man in fits of laughter. The man was in the pulpit and mum was looking up at him.

"Come and meet the vicar Freddie," mum shouted.

As I went over the man came down the small stairs from the pulpit, put out his hand and said "How do you do Freddie?"

He was very posh and definitely not from Liverpool.

Mum said, "Its ok Freddie this is Reverend Maximillian, (Max for short).

He is the vicar who my Mum works for as I shook his hand he gave me a smile and he seemed ok.

After a short while I got to know Max and he insisted I call him Max, but Mum said only when we were on our own, and that started to happen a lot. Max befriended Mum and me especially Mum at first. Max started coming for dinner at our house a lot, he would buy Mum real meat and then she would invite him to eat with us. Max never bothered much with my brothers and sisters; Mum said it was because they would not go to church. Something you have to understand, even though we now lived in a big house, Mum still had nine kids to feed, so Max buying food made a massive difference, and only I went to church with mum and that was not because I had suddenly found God, quite the opposite, if there was a God he took my Dad away from me, and I was still very angry, I went because our house was still a busy place and the only way I could get time with mum was to be in the kitchen, helping her with washing, ironing or cooking. Mum was at work or in the kitchen, so after Dad died, I started at the age of just ten years, learning how to run a kitchen and cook and go to church. Mum said it was a big help, I think it was the only way I could be close to my mum.

Mum didn't go to church for God either, it was because she got paid, and as we got to know people in church they treated our family as the widow and orphans' family,

"Oh how sad," they would say! And then give mum a bag of hand-me-down clothes, Max got very close to Mum and he helped to keep her happy, I think the whole house was happy without Dad, all except for me, I missed him so much and I could not think why no one would talk about him.

As Mum, did more and more work at the church and the vicarage, (the big house where Max lived next to the church), I got to know Max better and better, and Mum was very happy and we had real meat twice a week and on a Sunday if Max came for dinner we always had a big piece of beef, because Max always got it on a Saturday from the butcher for Mum.

One day when I was at the vicarage I was cleaning the rooms upstairs for my Mum as she was downstairs doing ironing, it was just about teatime after I finished school, the door of the vicarage slammed shut, and I heard Mum say, "Afternoon vicar".

She always called Max vicar, "it's a windy one today."

"Hi Lyn," he replied, "yes sorry about the door, I've got to get changed I have a wedding rehearsal at the church".

"Freddie is upstairs doing some dusting."

"Ok," he shouted as he made his way upstairs. I jumped because I wasn't dusting at all; Max had some photos on his bed they looked really good. I had never seen proper photos before. Max caught me but made out he hadn't.

"Sorry," I said and went to go downstairs.

"Don't go," Max said, "you can look at the photos while I get changed," and then opened a drawer and pulled out some more,

"Have you been to all these places?" I asked.

"Yes," he said as he sat next to me on the bed in his underpants.

"I will take you one day," he said.

"And mum and my brothers and sisters?" I let out all excited.

"No," he said, "it will be just me and you".

I thought that could be ok and said, "why just me Max?"

"Because you are very special Freddy," as he stood up and dressed himself in his underpants, first to the left and then to the right, almost as if he was doing it to impress me about how big he was, and I said to him "You are standing to attention like my brothers do".

"Yes," he said, "I am excited about taking you on a trip Freddie, but I need to get changed now I am running late, we can carry this talk on another time, it will be our secret, ok?"

"Yes," I said as I wondered where Max would take me; before I could shake a donkey's tale Max was ready.

"I will see you soon Freddie, you can look at the photos any time you want, I keep them in that bottom draw".

"Ok thanks," I said.

"Don't forget our secret."

"Ok," I said and with that he was gone and I took some of the photos and ran down the stairs to Mum.

"Mum, look at these pictures aren't they good?"

"Where did you get them from? Go and put them back right now."

"No mum Max said I could look at them."

"Ok," she said with a sigh, "you better put them back anyway".

"Max is going to take me on a trip one day, he said so and it is going to be our secret, so don't go telling anyone mum, ok?"

"Yes ok," she said with an unbelieving smile on her face, "put them back now Freddie, I have nearly finished".

"Ok Mum," I said as I ran upstairs.

All the way home I was so excited, the thought of going on a trip, I have only been on a trip once and that was with Mum and Dad and all the gang, I think we went to a caravan for a week in north Wales. The only part I remember, apart from making sand castles on the beach, was we were all walking along a county road over a canal bridge, I had a little dog, called Bruce, and this day it would not stop barking and it was making Dad very angry, so he picked up the dog by the scruff of the neck and threw it in the canal off the bridge. Well, I created so much that Dad got hold of me by the scruff of the neck and threw me off the bridge into the canal, well after all the commotion everything was ok, I had shut up. Bruce the dog had shut up and Dad was happy but I think all my brothers and sisters and Mum were in shock, it became a family story about how little Freddie learnt to swim, and it is a fact that I am a great swimmer, even if I say so myself.

* * *

Over time Max became a big part of our lives, just Mum and me, we saw him almost every day, he got Mum doing more and more work, and gave her lots of stuff for the family, he started to spoil me a lot, sweets from the shop and things, just insignificant things.

I asked mum one day, "Mum is Max going to be our new dad?"

"Good God no," she replied with a stern look on her face, "whatever gave you that idea, he is a Vicar".

"Ok, I just wondered," when I next saw Max I asked him, "Max are you going to be my new dad?"

"No Freddie, but don't worry about anything I will always look after you and your mum."

"Ok," I said, just wondered".

Max started taking me out on a Saturday in his car, Mum knew and was very happy for me, I could talk to Max about my real dad, and Max said he was in heaven with God, I didn't understand but somehow it made me feel good about my dad, Max had a sports car it was an MGB GT, whatever that was, and it went very fast and it was great fun on the country roads,

Max took me everywhere; when we went to the countryside Max would stop at a pub, always the same one, the Horse and Cart, it was ok and on nice days we could sit in the pub garden, Max had a pint of beer and I had a soda, and we would both have a packet of crisps each. It reminded me of my dad and the snooker club, Max and I became great pals. I knew he was my pal because he would put his arm around me all the time, it sort of made me feel good, like I used to feel with my dad.

One day on the way home from the pub – it was a lovely day – Max stopped the car on a country lane, and got out, "Come on Freddie," as he beckoned on me to follow him, he jumped a gate into a field and went behind a fence, as I followed him he took down his pants and said, "come on we need to pee".

I said to him, "I don't need to go".

As he got his willy out he said, "come on hold mine for me".

It was a bit strange I thought, "I don't hold my brothers they hold their own".

"Come on," he said, "it will be fun".

"Ok," I said then, "but you better not piss on my hand".

"Come and get hold of it you will see".

So I got hold of his willy then he said, "Stroke it up and down it will make me pee quicker," I just did as he asked and he got very hard, it was quite big.

I said to him, "that is bigger than all my brothers".

"Faster, Faster," he shouted, then with a big sigh all white sticky stuff started coming out of his willy.

"What is that?" I asked.

"Come here and take your shorts off and I will show you, I didn't know what to think, and he was being very nice, and he seemed very happy, so I did what he asked, he sat down on a big tree stump, and sat me on his knee, and started rubbing my willy. It never got as big as his and no stuff came out, but Max seemed very happy. We eventually got dressed and when we got in the car, he just kept on at me this is our secret Freddie you don't tell anyone, he seemed kind of edgy and I didn't know what was going on so I just agreed.

* * *

Well now you get the picture.

Now from that day forward Max got to see me as much as he could, I don't think he loved me although he told me many times, I don't think he in his sickness knew what love could be, seems strange. I knew my dad loved me more than life, but he never told me once, yet Max tells me all the time and I don't believe or feel it. Max was very kind to me, but only because I had become his sex toy, after that first time Max started taking me on holidays all on our own, the first was to the Isle of Rum, in the Hebrides. You could not get a more remote or secluded place, then it was to London to meet his mum and dad, except I never did meet them, because every time we went, they would be away somewhere. Max started teaching me a lot about sex, not in a good way, in a very dirty, cunning and calculated way. I think I sensed, what he was doing was wrong, but I didn't know how, that first time was when I was just ten years old, what did I know, I was just a thick, lazy and stupid kid, according to all my teachers at school.

* * *

I often wondered what would happen if I told someone, and Max would by now be seducing me and my mum, with endless gifts of kindness, always enough but never too much, especially with my mum.

If I was to tell anyone, who would I tell? Let's start with Mum, she was now getting a lot of financial help at home that made her life a lot easier, my brothers and sisters never spoke to me they were wrapped up in their own lives and never spoke to me about my dad, so why would I think I could talk to them about this? Because Mum was getting it easier, and Max was very clever at letting me know it would all stop if I told anyone, and how they would not understand, and I suppose out of it I was getting things that I liked.

* * *

After that first time Max took me away, everything was just touching. That holiday at the age of ten and a half years old was my full baptism into the world of sex. I am not going to go into gory detail, you will have to use your own imagination, but let me set the scene for you a little. A young boy on his own with a predator, pretending to be my father and my best friend and a man of the cloth, a man of God, being driven in a fast sports car hundreds of miles to the Hebridean Islands on the north-west coast of Scotland, going to probably the remotest island there; the Isle of Rum. Seven miles long and just one mile across at its narrowest point, a small crofter's farm, that had a visitors outbuilding, that's where we would stay for a whole week. The farmer and his wife were very old and both had a great suntan from burning peat on the fire because they could not get coal. It was the most beautiful place I had ever seen, just the farmer, his wife, Max and me, the six sheep dogs, two ponies, hundreds of sheep, beautiful sea eagles, seals, hundreds of rabbits, and no one to call me, thick, lazy and stupid. Beautiful weather, the biggest ocean I had ever seen, a golden sandy beach about two miles long, great big sand dunes, and just me and Max, what a dream playground for a young fatherless boy from Liverpool. A boy that loved animals more than people, a wonder world of outstanding natural beauty.

There was only one thing to take away the beauty; the sexual predator who got more and more hungry with every sex act I would be made to perform, he was very cleaver at making sure I got plenty of pleasure for myself, to counter balance the things he would make me do, cleverly stroking me at night as I was going asleep, with all the things, nasty things, that would happen to my Mum if anyone found out. I would dream in the night, a terrifying picture of me screaming out to a crowded street, but no sound coming out of my mouth, I was tied back and could not get away, nobody could hear my screams, and across the crowded street, I could see my Mum bound, so she could not cry out, her face covered in tears and blood, when I told Max of my nightmare, he said that it was a sign from God of what would happen to me and my Mum if anyone found out. Then he would always make sure we did something nice.

* * *

Sowing the seed of the beast

The overriding part of this story at this point, is that this is a so called man of the cloth, man of God, sowing seeds of the devil in the worst possible way, so that as you read on with this story, I can tell you that everything is fact right up to when I break free at the age of sixteen years of age. From then on, you will have some understanding of specific times in my life where the beast would grow. You will have to from this point on decide, using your own judgment, what if anything is fact and what if anything is fiction? Because the beast is very good at playing games in your mind, and the beast was given a masterclass and a university degree by a master craftsman of deceit, lies and fear, a disciple not of God, but the Devil; Max!

CHAPTER FOUR

The Second Predator

This is only the start of the abuse and rape, of a young boy from the city streets of Liverpool, who mourned after the death of his father! The vicar, Max, was the pastoral vicar in the local sea cadet corps, and managed to get me in at the age of 11 years, one year before I was legally meant to be there and he managed to get my mum in to make refreshments in the galley – that is the ships kitchen – on the outside everything looked normal, but the introduction to the sea cadets was to make my abuse much, much worse. I was introduced to a very powerful man, reportedly one of the richest men in the whole of Liverpool, Johnathan Jefferson Lawrence, he was commonly just know as JJ, this man was to make the work of Max look very small by comparison. JJ had the advantage of a mansion in a very affluent area of Liverpool, and a farmhouse in the beautiful mountains of Wales. The beauty would on many occasions be destroyed by the acts of abuse and continuous rape that would happen at the hands of Max and JJ. After every act would always come a reward, just the way you would train an animal, I was nastily trained, I didn't know any difference, this was my life for six years, the house in the city had a massive room at the top that was always locked, except when it was in use and JJ was the only key holder. What went on in this room is not something I can write about, but I will draw you a picture in your mind, then you can take it where you will.

As you walk up to the very top flight of stairs, the hall becomes very dark and the huge, door is hardly visible, it has a big padlock on it, then you need two big brass keys to open the top lock and the other to open the bottom lock. As the door is pushed open the first thing that you notice is how heavy the door is, there is a light switch on the left just as you step into the room. As you put the light on you then see the sign on the top of the door, (Welcome to the Dungeon) then the room is kited out with all sorts of frames, a swing suspended from the roof beams, but no ordinary swing, but one you can put all your arms and legs in and be suspended on your back or your front, to the far side of the room was a very luxurious sofa near to a drinks cabinet, loaded with everything you could think of, then scattered around the room was lots of equipment of every fashion, made out of the finest black leather, in fact everything in the room was made or dressed in the finest black leather. In the far right corner of the room there was a big screen, and a film projector on a table, fitted on the wall a cabinet with row after row of film reels, every one of them hardcore pornography, then scattered on the floor lots and lots of leather cushions of every size and colour. All around the room were scattered toy fury animal, there were leather whips, slapping straps, handcuffs, leather and rubber mouth gags, masks, lots of ropes of different lengths and sizes, and much, much more, including magazines and books, with diagrams and instructions of how to use everything, just in case you had no imagination.

The rest of the house was normal, but everything in the house was the finest of everything, all the finery you could imagine, then as the abuse and rape got worse and more frequent, Max and JJ did everything they could to keep my mouth shut and mum sweet. Mum's life definitely got better so I always did whatever I was asked. My brothers and sisters never knew anything, and they never missed me at all, I thought they never mentioned my dad, so why should they want to know anything about me.

Then there was my school, I would get very angry but no one wanted to know why, so on top of the attitude of being, thick, lazy and stupid, now was being added to that, 'bad tempered', so all through my school years, I was expected to get into trouble and into fights, that was who I was defined to be, so that was who I became, the school was quite disappointed that no matter what, I would not bunk off, little did they know I was petrified of my mum.

The school came up with a way of keeping me happier, I had permission that if I was in a class I didn't want to be in, and I could find a teacher to allow me into their class, then I could swap, so all my academic classes went out of the window and in came, woodwork, metalwork, sports of every kind, and of course swimming, something I was very good at, something no one in the school could come close to. The school had a great indoor swimming pool, so it wasn't a problem for me to get in almost any time I wanted.

It worked for me and it worked for them, the problem came with exams, well the answer for that for me was easy I just would not do anything, and if they tried to make me, we would have a full-on confrontation; let me give you an example.

Teacher, "Freddie you need to try and take this paper?"

Freddie, "Not a chance".

Teacher, "If you don't try I must stop your sports and your swimming".

Freddie, "If you do that I will throw my chair through the window".

And on and on it would go and eventually I got my way, so in those days the school had to put up with me until I was in the summer of my fifteenth birthday, then I was expelled from school, apparently that was the earliest by law a kid could be kicked out, so the first chance the school got they took it.

I feel I was completely let down by my school, not at the time, because I didn't know any different, that was just the way life was for me, but for many years as I struggled so much in an adult world, I felt so let down, not one person tried to find out what was wrong with me, not even in my family everyone else could read and write!

* * *

Summer of 1966.

This was my first introduction to the farmhouse in the Welsh mountains, could you imagine a house in 1966, having a cinema room? Well this one did and it was so posh, at the side of the cinema room was a dressing room with a communal shower, and hanging on the walls a whole row of one size fits all rubber all in one suits, very shiny and very sticky, with a vent at the front for your penis to come through. This was so as you watched pornographic films everyone could masturbate, usually each other, and now I was only twelve years old.

The rest of the house was made for entertaining at the highest level, and at the rear of the house a long wooden building that was a fully kitted out dormitory, that could sleep 22 people. With its own shower room and bathroom, the one thing that JJ made an issue of was the size and luxury in the communal showers and bath, every imaginable selection of fine toiletries and towels, dressing gowns and the like, well you can use your own imagination as to why. The estate as it was had a funny Welsh name that I don't think anyone except JJ could pronounce, and when all the kids from the sea cadets were there it was called an outward bound school, it was a fun place to be for most of the time, except night times and after the adults had been drinking their fine wines and cocktails, then for me they had to make sure the beast was being fed!

As the months and years went by, I quickly learnt that something was in my favour, because I could sense at times a nervousness with Max and JJ, that could almost be described as panic. I didn't realize fully the power that I had, when they felt the need to keep me in check and quiet, it always involved a bribe, and I always insisted that they looked after my mum.

Max would give Mum a bonus for the work she did and JJ would bring around great big food hampers. Mum never knew the real reason why she was getting all this stuff, and I wish now I'd had the nerve to insist on a lot more. I think one year in the summer holidays JJ said I would be working as a waiter in his restaurant, it was in the city and so posh you could not get your breath. I was there to learn everything about silver service, I was 13 years old and I thought it was a real treat, little did I know that it was just the next stage of my grooming, I had to tell everyone I was JJ's nephew and that I was 16 years old. It was good learning how all that posh stuff worked and I quickly became very good at it, and I was being paid, five shillings and sixpence a week. I had work cloths hand made for me and I did look the part, even if I say so myself.

Well the real reason for all this polishing up was, now JJ had his own personal waiter and butler, I think he would have had me driving his Rolls-Royce if I had been older, and once again I will have to leave you to your own imagination as to all the extra duties I would be asked to perform. Now at the age of 14 years, I would be with Max during the week, because mum would not let me miss school, and with JJ and his friends at the weekend, and on school holidays.

Then after I was expelled from school, my mum said to me, "Right Freddie you need to get a real job now if you want to stay under my roof."

Well I could have easily moved in with JJ but I had grown to know that all that stuff was not right, even if I could not get out of it, so I got a job on a building site making the tea for all the workers, after all I was now fully trained in silver service. JJ was fuming mad, but my mum was so happy, she called it real work, as I started to get to know people at work, some of the lads nearer to my age, asked me why I was so angry all the time, and I have to say I was. Obviously I could not tell them, some off the lads said to me I would be good in the boxing ring and took me to the local boxing club, it was really good for getting my anger out, and I was now at this stage seeing less of Max and JJ and more of my mates at work and at the boxing club. So much so that I wanted to know about women, I went out on the town with the lads from work and I remember it well, just before my sixteenth birthday, the lads said they would fix me up with a good women to sort out my cherry, well I didn't know what that meant, but as the night unfolded, I was to find out. The girls name was Mandy and she really showed me what life was all about, I told Max and JJ and said to JJ we should have women at his house, well yes I was a little naïve still.

Well the suggestion went down like a lead balloon, one of the men at work I thought was a good friend asked me where I lived and for some stupid reason I told him I lived with my rich uncle, in a big posh house, this pal to be was called Paul and he didn't believe me at all so one weekend when JJ was away I invited Paul and a couple of local prostitutes up to JJ's house. I had a spare key and I knew the alarm code, so we were all set, we had some booze, some women and then on Monday Paul would think I was the bee's-knees. Well that Saturday everything was set, I had got in the drinks and some food so that JJ wouldn't know anything, and Paul came with the girls, Paul turned up with four girls and I was so excited, I could hardly get my pants on, I took everyone up to the room at the top of the house, and from then on you will have to let your imagination work out the rest, it was about eight pm and everything was going great. We had all got a little drunk when at about 11.30pm JJ came home unexpectedly, with some men who I didn't know, well a right ding-dong started, with me trying to tell JJ they were my friends and insisting I had every right because he had said this could be my home, Paul and the girls went crazy, the girls screaming that JJ and his friends were faggots and they would call the police, about all the stuff in the house. I didn't know what to do as I insisted that Paul and the girls must leave, after some persuasion they left, the girls insisted we paid them for the whole night, and some extra to shut them up, then I had to get it off JJ and all the time he was having a go at me. I could feel my temper getting stronger and stronger, one of JJ's friend's started shouting at JJ, "throw the little beggar out JJ, or give him to me and I shall rip the backside out of him". Well that was it, the red mist finally came down and I got a hold of this guy, who's name I didn't even know, and I gave him a battering, the like of which he had never known. When I was finished, he was in need of an ambulance, JJ told me I had better go home, but now I had got brave I had at last let all the rape and abuse for the past six years, explode. I started shouting at JJ why don't you call the police and tell them what has happened? I knew he wouldn't, because I had learnt enough by now that what he and Max had been doing to me would have got them both in a lot of bother, I didn't really know how much bother, but I had an inkling it would be bad enough. Well the only thing stopping me at that point was that I didn't want my mum and family to find out, so JJ rang for an ambulance and he also rang Max to come and get me.

When the ambulance arrived JJ's friend was in the street and said he had been attacked in the street by a gang of thugs, and that JJ had kindly rang for the ambulance, so no police came, shortly afterword's Max arrived in a bit of a panic asking what had gone on. He was more concerned that he didn't get dragged into anything and that he only had a few hours before he had to be in church. Well they decided that Max should take me to his house and let everything calm down, and that JJ would come and get me in the afternoon once he had sorted his friend out at the hospital. I suddenly realized that they were both very nervous, and as I was still all fired up I said to them both, "this is what is going to happen I am going back with Max and he is going to drop me around the corner from my mum's house, then on Monday my mum is going to get a big fat bonus for some extra work I did over the weekend. Then after I finish work on Monday night you will meet me with a lot of money, and it had better be enough to keep me quiet for a very long time, very nervously they both agreed, on the way home with Max not a word was spoken, and all of a sudden I felt I had a lot of power and I liked it. I finally got to my Mum's house about 5am, Mum went mad at me soon as I got in the door, she could see I was in a state, I just told her I got in a bit of trouble in town.

I could not sleep everything spinning around in my head and none of it was making any sense. When I got up in the morning – well it was more like early afternoon – everyone was trying to find out what had gone on, but my temper was raging and I bit everyone's head off. It was a difficult day, I went to work and when I saw Paul, right away he asked me right up front, "did I know those guys were faggots?" I just fronted him up and said don't be daft JJ's my uncle, and it seemed to work, but I was very nervous, confused and angry. Well, in the evening mum told me that she had got a very big bonus from the vicar, and apparently, it was due to all my challenging work over the weekend, and that I was to go to the vicar as he had something for me.

* * *

Later in the evening I went around to see Max, he had £500 in a big envelope for me and said don't go to JJ's house any more. I was shocked by the amount of money, I was only expecting about £50, I gave Max JJ's house keys and went back home, the next day I didn't go into work, in fact I never went back to work at all and about a week later, I went to the Royal Navy recruiting office and signed up for nine years. I was only a few months off my sixteenth birthday, that would be 8 September 1970 and I could join on 5 November that same year, I just had to get my mum to come with me to the Royal Navy office and sign the forms to say she was happy for me to go.

I was very apprehensive in telling mum as we had not been getting on so well, in fact I wasn't getting on with anyone, and I was losing my temper all the time with everyone. I was now getting very bold, and I had been working out at the boxing club, I told mum about the Royal Navy and I was shocked she was so happy for me and could not get to the Royal Navy office quick enough, Mum said it would be the making of me.

* * *

I still had some money left and I hadn't seen JJ for some time, I saw Max in church when I went with my mum but Max was very distant, the amount of money JJ had given me kept going round and round in my head, and I was beginning to realize, that Max and JJ were frightened what I might do, I was now just four weeks from joining the Royal Navy, and one night when I had a few drinks, I got very bold and went and knocked JJ's door. He was entertaining at the time and he was shocked to see me/

"I am busy what do you want?" he said in a very stern voice.

"I am joining the Royal Navy in four weeks," I replied.

"I know Max had told me, what do you want?"

"Well I thought about going and having a talk with the police to let them know what had been going on in my life, what do you think?"

JJ looked very panicked and said, "Look come and see me in the morning about 11am,"

"You had better have £2,000 for me," I replied.

The next morning I was at JJ's house bang on time, and even though I was being very bold I was crapping myself, I was actually shaking as I walked up his drive way, that was a measure of how rich he was, he had a drive way, well I took a deep breath and rang the bell. JJ was very composed, and invited me in, and started making small talk, about what I was going to do in the Navy, I just replied to him, "getting away from you and Max, and believe me you are both getting off light." JJ gave me an envelope with the money in it, I didn't count it I was shaking and could not wait to get out.

* * *

I took the money and I was off. I went to the nearest pub and locked myself in one off the toilets to count the money, I was shocked there was £2,500 in the envelop, and I was dancing, I was also trembling as I had never seen that much money, I had a pint and then went home and stashed the money away. My emotions were all over the place, I was excited and frightened, I wanted to tell the whole world how rich I was, and then I didn't want to tell a soul. As the weeks went by I very nearly didn't go in the Royal Navy, but then how would I explain to my mum. Well, finally the big day came and I had a one way travel warrant to HMS Woodrow in the very south of England near to the south coast, I had never been that far before. Mum and everyone wanted to come to the train station to see me off, but I talked them into saying goodbye at the house, 10.15 from Lime Street Station, Liverpool to Portsmouth and I was on my way, even as I was stepping on the train I was thinking am I doing the right thing, my driving force was I am finally rid of Max and JJ, little did I know how much emotional damage had been done!

* * *

I had wanted to open a bank account but was afraid there would be too much talk about the money, so before I left home, I stuffed some of it down my sock, just £30 and the rest I wrapped up in lots of newspaper and tied string around it, then when no one was about I got into the loft and hid the package where no one could find it.

The next morning, I was ready to go everyone was up and ready to see me off, Mum was the only one who gave me a hug, and I could see she had tears in her eyes, I didn't hang about. Mum had given me Dad's old navy holdall bag, I didn't have much in it as I was told we would get given everything we needed.

So I was off and on my way, the train journey was ok I had butterfly's in my stomach all the way down, I didn't talk to anyone I was just looking out of the window dreaming about all the places I could go to, and that I was following in my Dads footsteps. I had such a mix of emotions going on inside me, many times I thought I would get off the train and go home, but I knew there would be a huge commotion and I would not be able to explain things. But the biggest reason for not going back was that I was now free from Max and JJ, and that meant so much to me. I kept telling myself I could get through anything now after surviving the past six years of abuse and rape. I got to Portsmouth and there were people to meet us with a bus to take us to HMS Woodrow, some lads were already on the bus, I was told to find a seat and we were just waiting for two more people to arrive, I got on the bus but didn't speak to anyone, then before long everyone was on the bus and we were off on the next part of the journey. Some lads tried to introduce themselves to me but I put up a barrier, I think they thought I was homesick, I was far from it I was at last free, and all I could think about was how proud my dad would be where ever he was.

**

I knew he was not with any God, because if there was a God he certainly didn't do me any favours. Letting me go to a church to be abused and raped, I will keep on saying raped because that is what it was; RAPE! Somehow, I kept wondering if I had stashed my money away in a good place, what if there was a house fire no one would know the money was there? How could I let my Mum know without lots of questions?

"Ok you lot off the bus fall in outside, lines of three." I can hear boys saying what does this guy mean, and why does he keep shouting at the top of his voice? Little did they know what was coming, I responded so quick the other boys must have thought I went from being asleep, to being struck by lightning. Well they could be right, I had spent five years in the sea cadet corps, and I knew a Royal Marine Sergeant Major's voice when I hear one, I was off the bus like a shot, first on the parade ground, bag in front and standing forming the first line. I looked straight in front of me and never flinched. Right away one off the assisting chiefs stood right in front of me, shouting, "come on you grubby pile of shits, fall in on my left" and he held out his pace stick in order to give direction, he then said to me, "what is your name" looking me straight in the eye, I sprung to attention and shouted at the top of my voice, "Freddie Sir".

He replied to me, "do you see any fancy officers' badges on me you cocky little shit?"

"No sir, I mean no chief," then he looked to his left' my right.

"Come on you grubby lot, fall in, fall in," once we were all together we were marched off to our dormitories, names taken, bed allocations, uniforms and then we were fed, watered and put to bed, lights out at 10pm – 22.00hrs.

Talk about a gang of school kids on a high that night, I interrupted the antics and high spirits to say, "you all need to get some sleep, you will need it, reveille will be at 6am sharp and we will have a full days training in front of us," well eventual the girls settled down and we all got some sleep.

CHAPTER FIVE

Royal Navy Training

We were under initial training for 12 weeks and it was going to be a big slog, in lots of ways. I was miles ahead the others because of the training from the sea cadets and obviously Max and JJ. When the boys were talking about girls – that was almost every night – I was very much left out as I had no experience with them, and most of the boys were one or two years older than me. One of them Geordie – he was called that because he was from Newcastle – he was 19 years old and the oldest in the troop, there were a few guys a little younger than me, but only by weeks or months, I soon learnt the talk about women, and before long I was an expert.

I was very good at doing all the uniforms and boots at the end of the day because I knew what I was doing, so I soon got the job of helping people catch up, it was good because it made me feel wanted in a very normal way and not because of what people wanted to do with me. We could not get any leave for the first six weeks and we had to score enough merit points to qualify for our first night off the camp. So I was good at getting everyone up to scratch, every time I scored points for one of the other lads, they would owe me a pint of beer, that was my price, they were all puzzled, as to why I charged a pint of beer as I think I was the only one that drank alcohol, the age in those days to drink legally was 21 years old, and as that was none of us I had them scratching their heads just a little. I had been drinking in pubs since I was thirteen years old.

One of the tasks we had to learn during our marching drills was the ceremonial dressing of the mast.

Let me explain.

At one end of the parade ground was an old square rig mast, one hundred and twenty-seven feet high to the top of the button on the top. The button was an eight inch diameter piece of wood fixed to the very top of the mast, then coming down in succession there were three horizontal booms and rigging, that in the days of old, the sails would be fixed to. The process was simple, during our passing out parade, we would have to climb the mast going in order of age, the youngest going to the very top, to stand on the button and salute, all in time to the music that the Royal Marine Band would play, and then in turn we would all stand on the booms and rigging, in order to get the training just right, every evening at sunset we would practice the drill so that by the end of our training it would be perfect.

So having spent most of my time in training getting other lads up to scratch, with regard to washing, ironing and the old spit and polish on the boots, half way through when we were let on leave for a Saturday night, I called in all my chips from the lads. I got drunk, paid for a prostitute and then got into a fight on the way back to camp, I got back about two minutes before the end of our curfew at 22.00hrs and I managed to stand up straight as I went through the guardroom, two of the lads slightly distracted the duty officer so I could get through without any questions, job done!

We made it to the end of the training and I had made my mark as being fearless and a tough nut to crack, just what the Navy wanted in those days, the only down side was my reading and writing. On the next part two specialists training I had to take evening classes to get my basic academic skills to a reasonable level, this would be something I would always struggle with. I told you about the ceremonial climbing of the mast, the button boy at the top of the mast always had to be the youngest recruit so that wasn't me and I was desperate to get to the top of the mast. Well on our passing out day all the families came, except mine and everyone was allowed leave with their family members after the parade. I didn't go as I would have been on my own, so I had smuggled a bottle of rum onto the camp and began a party all on my own, it was about 21.00 hrs or 9 pm and I was about half way through the bottle of rum, and I had a great idea. As no one was about

I would climb the mast on my own and stand on the button, perfect I thought as I sneaked my way onto the parade ground and over to the mast. It looked a lot taller than in the daytime, with just a few floodlights at the bottom and no music to keep the count as we went up, one big deep breath and I'm off, singing my own tune as I ascended the mast. Halfway up the first part of the rigging and everything is fine, I make it to the half-moon that's about three quarters of the way up, now up the Jacobs ladder just the shimmy up the last bit of the pole, swing myself around onto the button stand to attention the band stops playing and then I salute.

Just as I get my salute in there is an almighty bellow from the ground, "well done Mak'a" that's what they call me now, "get your ass down from there and report to me in your number one uniform at the guard house in five minutes."

Oh shit I thought to myself and there was no need to ask who that was shouting up at me, I would know the Fleet Master-at-arms voice anywhere. I was down the longest rope and at the bottom in a flash into my number one's (best uniform) in the next flash and reporting to the duty officer in four minutes and fifty-five seconds.

"A good job you have already passed out," the number one said exasperatedly at me.

"Yes sir" was my reply, with my half bottle of rum about to come up and make an appearance.

"What shall I do with you Mak'a?" he mutters at me.

"String you up from the yard arm in Drake's day my lad."

"Yes sir," I reply, wondering if my rum is going to stay down and whatever is going to come next.

"First thing in the morning, before breakfast, I want you to report to the duty chief of the watch and he will give you ten laps of the parade ground as you like it here so much" "yes sir" I reply as he lets me go, I just made it back to my billet in time for the rum to make an appearance, well safe to say I got through all that and made it to my next stage of training at

HMS Cornwallis, at RNAS Sea-shanty in the south west a Royal Navy Airfield Station.

* * *

I was now a naval airman and the first week was labelled for us as familiarization and awareness, this place was massive and there were aircraft and helicopters flying around all day from first light to sunset and sometimes even into the evening. We were given all the rest of our uniforms and equipment, there was even our own bus service so we could get around the camp and the airfield. Once again our leave was restricted for the first six weeks, and because of our age we could not move around on our own, we were allocated sea daddies, these were men that would chaperone us everywhere we went. Our billet or bunk house had room for twenty new recruits, us and four sea daddies, everywhere we went we had to march as one body of men, and just about everyone on the barracks had an eye on us in case we did anything wrong.

It was four weeks before we could get onto the airfield itself and that was another leave of training. It had already been established that I could not read or write properly, so I was given extra classes in the education department, for reading, writing and maths. I was given a warning that I had to come up to scratch very quickly or I would be back classed and the rest of my recruitment would go on to the next level without me. I had already established myself as a bit of a loner so that was no threat to me, I was good at working in a group only when I had to, otherwise I would be on my own. In our off duty time we could go to the NAFFI, that had a big function room and bar, shops and a cinema, then there were recreation rooms with TV's, snooker and pool tables, darts and every board game invented. You can guess I would spend most of my time playing snooker, and just like my Dad I was good, not just good, I was the best. A short walk from the camp, about 40 minutes away was the beach, also on the camp were several wait training rooms, skipping ropes and a fully equipped boxing ring.

I was soon isolating myself at every opportunity and becoming very fit and angry, it wasn't long before the other lads as soon as work was finished would leave me out of everything and it was ok by me.

Part one of our training was coming to an end and the inevitably was about to happen, I was back classed to the new recruitment intake. I wasn't bothered it meant I knew what was to come for the next twelve weeks, the only difference was the subjects I had done well at I didn't have to do again, instead I had to spend more time on my reading writing and maths. My isolation was not going unnoticed by the instructors, one weekend one of my new class mates made the mistake of confronting my beast, he was a big lad and he came to my space at the end of the bunk house with a few lads behind him.

"Scouse," his said, that's what everyone called me because I was from Liverpool, "aren't you the guy that climbed the mast on your own at HMS Woodrow?"

"Yes," I said in reply.

"Well how come you can do all that and you can't read and write?" he had a smile on his face and I could feel the beast making his move inside me, and as they mocked me some more and began to have a good laugh at my expense, all I could see was my teachers at school laughing in the same way saying I was thick, stupid and lazy, and slapping me across the back of my head or my ear. As the guys in my bunk house continued I could feel the teachers slaps and I was physically flinching, then the beast took control of me fully, I was burning up inside, and I heard this guy say, "what are you flinching for Scouse," and it seemed like ever one was laughing. They kept on and on then I could not see the guys, I saw Max and JJ laughing at me, the next thing was I woke up in the guardhouse in a cell, there was a leading airman and a doctor looking over me, I was relieved the beast had gone.

"Good you are awake," the doctor said, "I don't know what happened, do you want to tell me?"

I never said a word, and he asked several times, I still kept my silence, mostly because I didn't know.

"Well you are fit to be detained and you will be up before the Captain on Monday morning."

"What for?" I asked.

"Well young man, you have put three men in my sick bay".

That's the camp hospital. It was ok in the guardhouse but the men that were on duty to guard me were very standoffish. I thought to myself I suppose the beast did an excellent job then, I wasn't worried the beast had started to give me an inner attitude that nothing was relevant. After all what was the worst that could happen? Nothing in comparison to what Max and JJ had done. I had become very good at enjoying my own company. At least in the guardhouse I had my own shower and toilet, I have always had a problem taking a communal shower, I'd leave it to be the very last or get up before everyone else and get in first.

On the Monday morning my divisional officer came to see me, "Morning Mak'a you have had fun by the sounds of it, what happened?"

"I don't know sir," I couldn't tell him about the beast; I would have to spill the beans on everything.

"Don't give me that," he said, "It is my job this morning to defend you before the Captain's table."

"Honestly sir, I just don't know."

"Well I can tell you that if we don't come up with something then you will have the book throne at you."

I was taken under guard to my billet to get changed into my number one uniform, the other lads were there but no one was allowed to say anything, when I was marched into the captain's table by the Fleet Master-at-Arms, the order was given off caps as the charge was read out, three counts of assault, disorderly conduct and bringing dishonour to my uniform, "how do you plead," said the officer of the day.

"Guilty sir," I answered. I didn't see any other way because I didn't know what the beast had done.

The Captain hesitated and said to my section officer, "Do you have anything say on behalf of Naval Airman Mak?"

"No sir," he answered, then the Fleet Master-at-Arms said, "there are three witnesses sir".

"Let's hear what they have to say".

The first one was marched in, then the next and then the last one, the big guy who started the problem, they all had black eyes and the big guy had a broken nose. Inside I could feel the beast laughing at them, when each of them spoke they all stated that it was their fault and I was not to blame for the fight. Well at the end of the day we were all found guilty of disorderly conduct, we were all fined two weeks wages and 14 days extra duties. The extra duties are called (number nines, or nines,) I had to do my extra duties in the galley – that's the main kitchens – and I had to start at 0400hrs every morning for 14 days. I didn't mind at all because I had enjoyed being in my mum's kitchen, when I first went in it was massive, and every morning I had to do three hours on the pot wash, a little different to mum's kitchen.

After being back classed things went much better, all the lads stood well back from me and the trainers saw two things of interest,

1. I could not be broken by extra work, the more they worked me, the harder they road my back, the stronger I got.
2. I could look after myself and I had no fear, they had met the beast. In the months and years to come the Navy would make effective use of both things. You see in the armed forces if you had a bad temper, they would not want to break you from that, they would want you to keep it and teach you how to make it useful. The thing was, all the time they did not know that the driving force was the beast inside me, the manipulated training was playing right into the hands of the beast.

I very quickly learnt how to manipulate most situations so that the beast and me got the best of both worlds. We were soon standing out, for being first in everything, we would be the first to volunteer for everything, regardless as to what it was, and if I could not negotiate into a place of advantage, then we would be more than happy to bully and frighten people so we got what we wanted. The beast and me became so physically fit not one person would take us on, and we was full of ourselves with it, the other side of the coin was not one single person liked us. We would never be invited to social events, and it was fine with me and the beast, when it was time to be part of a team that was fine, we could do that, but whatever team we would be a part of they would just have to put up with us. I anyone in a team tried to make us look bad, they all knew there would be serious consequences, the people that got to know us the most was the Fleet Master-at-Arms, he was the one that kept discipline on every ship, and the Captain, who would always be giving out my punishment, which happened a lot.

CHAPTER SIX

My First Ship

My how time goes by, I have got through all my training, and I am now waiting for 'Drafty', that's the name for the drafting officers, to sort me out a post or a ship. They ask what your preference might be, not that you would get it, but they do ask? Most of the guys, want more training, more exams, they say it's the best way of getting promotion and working your way through the ranks. Well I have got news for them, me and the beast will find a way. I told Drafty, "Just give me a ship that is sailing as far from the UK as I can get.

Part of my training was learning how to drive, we started with Land Rovers, then seven and a half ton trucks, then onto 30 ton trucks, then articulated trucks, and finally airfield fire engines. It was great fun and something I am very good at. I was in driver training for sixteen weeks, so my very first post was as a driver on the fire station, one of the other areas of training I was good at, fire's never scared me. I had a great natural respect, it was like a fire and the beast had something in common, they both needed to be fed, the only difference was with a fire, no matter how big it got, you could always find a way to put it out, but with the beast it would just now and again go to sleep, but it could never be extinguished, and when it woke up after a sleep, it would be really hungry. After it had been fed, usually followed by a visit to the Fleet Master-at-arms and the Captain.

I asked why I could not get a ship right away and apparently it was my age, I could not go to sea until I was 18 years old, otherwise they would need my mum's permission. Don't be getting confused now, the age of consent at this time was still 21 years, it was just that anything like going out of the country they would need Mum's written consent, so to avoid all that bother they put me on the fire station. Once again I was made to be an outsider, or should I say, I made myself an outsider, I just didn't want boys or men to come anywhere near me, and I let them know it, I started to realize that the frequency that I was ending up in front of the Captain was not doing me any good in getting my drafting to a ship. I was three months away from my 18th birthday, and I didn't want to stay on the airfield a day longer than I had to.

One of my chief petty officers, came to me and said, "Scouse do you want to get a sea draft?"

"Yes chief," I replied, "more than anything".

"Can you drive?" he asked.

"Yes chief," I answered in an excited manor.

"I cannot give you any promises but I know the *Royal-Alexander* has nearly finished refit; you birthday is early September isn't it?"

"Yes chief."

"I might be able to get you on the crash and salvage unit, it's only a very small unit with a total of six men and an officer".

"Yes please chief."

"Ok, you will have to keep away from the Fleet Master-at-Arms, and no more visits to the Captain's table."

"No problem, Chief."

"The *Royal-Alexander* sails for sea trials and warm ups at the end of September, then goes on an around the world trip for eighteen months, ok?"

"Yes Chief, you won't get a whisper out of me."

"And one more thing, keep this information to yourself."

"Yes chief."

I was so excited I could have bust a gut; my first thought was how do I keep the beast under control? I planned I would just do my work each day, I would volunteer for extra duties, and not go ashore at all, I could keep myself supper fit, and out of trouble. People around me noticed a big change and some even got bold enough to ask what was going on. I just smiled and said nothing, after about six weeks my station officer called me in his office and before he could get a word in, I burst out.

"Look sir, I have done nothing wrong ok."

"I know you haven't, I called you in to say I had noticed a great change in your attitude and want you to keep it up."

"Ok sir," and I was out of his office like a shot, I had no respect for the man and wasn't going to let him get in the way of my draft to the *Royal-Alexander*.

Well the day finally arrived three days after my birthday, I was called into the station officer I was trembling, "Well naval airman Mak, it seems I am finally getting rid of you, you have got a draft to the *HMS Royal-Alexander*, you have to report to the Fleet Master-at-Arms this afternoon and he will give you all your papers".

"Yes sir, thank you sir," me and the beast were dancing.

* * *

Later that afternoon I reported to the Fleet Master-at-Arms, he made me wait outside his office for over an hour, I knew it couldn't be much longer because he lived off the camp and he would be going home to his wife, the door opened and a loud voice that was unmistakable bellowed out, "ok Mak'a, get your backside in here".

I march in and stood to attention, "Yes sir".

"Well young man I have two files here, this one," as he lifted it up and banged it down on the table, was quite a thick file, "this is your disciplinary records, and this one is your drafting orders," and he kept it in his hand in the air, "your orders are to travel by train on the 11.25hrs train to Port Andrew and report to the regulating officer on board the *HMS Royal-Alexander*. Now it remains if I will let you go, Bearing in mind the size of your discipline file, what do you say to that. Now I was really shaking, at first I could feel the beast rising in me and in a flash I was thinking if he stops me I will probably kill him.

Then he said, "Come on then, what have you got to say for yourself".

I don't know where the answer came from but in reply I said, "Yes sir all my fault, sir I don't deserve a break, and you would be quite right in stopping my draft sir, but in my defence sir I think in the last three months I have proved I can change sir, and I really think you want to get rid of me, sir."

"You are one cheeky son of a bitch Mak'a, and you are right I do want rid of you. So I am putting this file in my desk, because if I send that with you, you won't get up the gangway, so in your drafting reports I have put in a report based on your last three months, but let me warn you I know the Fleet Master-at-Arms on the *Royal-Alexander*, he is a good pal of mine, and I will be keeping a good check on you. If you falter in any way, this file might catch up with you, do you understand?"

"Yes sir."

I had my drafting papers and I was out like a shot, as I was about to leave I just could not go without having the last word, "is that a little smile I see their sir?"

He jumped up kicked me up the backside and said, "Get out Mak'a before I change my mind," and as he was closing the door I could hear him having a little chuckle to himself.

HMS Royal-Alexander, Port Andrew

Day one; this ship is massive, the biggest aircraft carrier of the Royal Navy, I get escorted to my mess deck, which is where I will live and have my time off duty, for the next year and a half. The first thing that struck me in all my excitement, is how small everything is in the mess deck, I am introduced to the leading hand of the mess deck, and as he is talking to me the excitement is changing to something else, the beast is not happy. 120 men in the smallest of spaces you could imagine, the shower room is just four toilets, four urinals, and four showers, then I was shown to my bunk space, this is your bedroll I am told, and this is your locker.

"You will soon get used to everything,"
I'm not sure, I think to myself, the beast inside me is really struggling, so many men so close together. I am taken then to meet my new sea daddy, he looks ok, and he then starts to show me around the ship. He first takes me to where I will work on the flight deck, we walk over to a great big, mobile crane, and when I say big, I mean huge.

"It is undergoing a service at the moment, so you won't be able to drive it for about four days or so, that will give you time to get to know your way around first."

How the heck am I going to drive that thing, it was called jumbo, the right name for it! Well as the beast and me start to get settled in, the jumbo has finished its service and the chief of my section instructs me to put it through its paces.

"Is someone going to show me how first?" I asked.
Well there was a mighty explosion from my section chief, "You mean you haven't been trained on the Jumbo".
"No chief, I was only asked if I could drive, I wasn't asked what can I drive."

Well there was some trouble now, the ship is sailing in five days and there is no time to get a replacement for me, I thought this would be the shortest draft for certain, after some time and many phone calls, it was decided I would go back to HMS Cornwallis, at RNAS Sea-Shanty and be trained on the jumbo there. This is the good bit, I was told to pack a bag for a couple of days, and report to the flight deck officer, they only took me in a sea king helicopter back to Sea-Shanty, for a crash driving course in how to drive the jumbo, this was where the only other jumbo in the world existed. It was great fun and the instructors had my full attention, whilst I don't read and write well, when it comes to manual things I am a supper fast learner, and my eye to hand skills are exceptional.

Well after two days I was back on a sea king helicopter and back on the *Royal-Alexander,* then before I had time to think we were on our way out to sea. Me and my opposite number, drove the jumbo and the three fixed cranes on each side of the ship, so when he was on duty I was off and when he was off I was on, when we came into port we would both be on duty as there would always be lots of work to do, I was doing well because I was more or less my own boss, the chief of the unit would give me instruction as to what had to be done, but before long I could anticipate his every move, and he got used to just letting me get on with it. There was some difficulty in the mess deck, it took the beast a long time to settle down, and the lads I had to share this tiny space with quickly learnt to give me and the beast plenty of space, the Fleet Master-at-Arms on the ship had a very good way of sorting out differences between people, in his office he had two pairs of boxing gloves, and any disputes were settled in the boxing ring. This suited me and the beast and before long there were not many people that would take us on. Once again this gave the powers that be, the driving force in the Royal Navy, a view of a very young man that had the persona of being reckless and fearless, I know now these are traits they look for, for them to make use of you, especially if you have little or no contact from your family members.

So, what are the sort of things they would look for I hear you ask? Well when you are being watched you never really know you are being watched, you only find out much, much later. In fact in my case it was many years later, what they look for is if you are a team player and if you can fit into a team, for me I could not only fit into a team, I would very quickly lead the team, usually because early on in the team I would do something that would scare the pants off the team. The thing with a team is this, you all have to work together especially in training, and if one failed the whole team failed, so if they complied with me they quickly realized that whatever we would be taxed to do would not only be done well but we would always, without fail, come first or score the most points.

Another thing the people watching would look for was if I could do things on my own initiative, this I was even better at because I had already formed the opinion that I was invincible, and nothing in the world could beat me. If you were to ask me if I was suicidal, my answer would be, "no but I had no fear of death," this made me totally reckless. The navy training very quickly controlled my recklessness and moulded it into controlled recklessness. I was observed for my contact with my family members, this was virtually none; my family didn't want to know my dad and never told me where he was buried, so why would I want to know them, and besides that when I came away from home I never had a single goodbye, and they never expected a letter because they knew I could not read or write, about once a year I would get a letter from my Mum short just asking if I was ok, no news of any kind, so what I would do is get someone to write a letter for me, or write as if it was a friend writing on my behalf.

Finally, we are on our way out to sea, it's very early in the morning and there is a slight sea mist in the air, it was almost as if we were sneaking out under the mist, then after about two hours, there was no land to be seen in any direction, I was so excited and the sea breeze on my face, the salt smell of the air is something I will never forget.

Our section chief came on the flight deck where the jumbo station was and announced, "ok everyone, shortly we are going to full flying stations, to get all our aircraft on board, so be alert because for some of these pilots it is the first time they will be landing on the ship in real time."

I felt the breeze coming over the flight deck getting stronger, the chief said "turn on your headsets" our headsets consist of a big belt with a radio receiver linked to my helmet that had ear phones in it, when we turned them on we could hear all the radio traffic between the aircraft the flight deck commander, his officers and staff, and the pilots of the aircraft, all of a sudden there was an announcement, "Flying stations, flying stations, this is not a drill, this is not a drill, flying stations, flying stations."

Then I could feel the ship turning hard to port, and the wind over the flight deck got even stronger, I was sitting on my jumbo and I had a fantastic view of the flight deck, then another announcement, "This is flight control, stand by to receive aircraft." I looked aft that's towards the back of the ship, and in the far distance I could see a tiny light, then another and another, as the first light got closer I could see the aircraft. I was excited it was a Buccaneer, I had seen them at sea shanty, now I am seeing them land on my ship, how crazy is that? I don't know who is the most excited the beast or me, or our section chief, you should see his face, (Oh no you can't it's my story) well you should see it, what a picture. After the Buccaneers are all on board safely then came the phantoms, the two gannets, and then the helicopters, it took all day and nearly into the night, and eventually the message came, "all hands stand down from flying stations, stand down".

That meant we could relax and take our time off, there was an electrifying buzz all over the ship, the section chief said to me stow everything away and we will all have a cup of tea, yes you are right I had to make the tea. I asked the chief, "How often do we go to flying stations?"

"Every day and even into the nights and sometimes even all night."

I was on such a high, as the days and weeks went by I soon got the hang of everything I needed to do, and me and my opposite number had to decide who was on what shift, so he took 06.00hrs to 18.00hrs and I took 18.00hrs to 06.00hrs, 12 hours on 12 hours off, that suited me ok.

I loved the night shift, it was so special seeing the stars at night, and then when we would be at flying stations, seeing the aircraft taking off at night was something so special, as the aircraft reach the end of the flight deck the pilots would put the nose of the aircraft up into the sky, then fire the afterburners and disappear into the night sky like a shooting star, it didn't matter how many times I saw that, every time was special.

* * *

Now a message comes around the ship that we needed to withdraw artic clothing from the main ships stores, because we were headed into the northern polar region, as we drew closer and the sea got so bad, I was surprised how such a big ship could get tossed around by the sea, at times the waves must have been eighty feet high, we would still go to flying stations, and it was such an art for the flight deck officers not to launch the aircraft into the belly of a wave, the timing every time had to be perfect, so spectacular. There would be no night flying as that was just a little too dangerous, it seemed like everyone was on extra duties, smashing the ice off the weather decks and the flight deck, the night skies were even more spectacular, it was as if the sky and its amazing colours was dancing, the further north we got the better the performance, we saw some icebergs, the sort that sunk the *Titanic* many years ago, lots of whales, and just as we are all getting used to our surroundings, we get told we are now to head off to the Mediterranean sea.

I didn't have a clue where that was, but all the lads said we could get a good suntan, and we might even get some shore leave, I couldn't imagine me and the beast putting our feet on foreign soil. As we started to sail south, the sea calmed down and the weather got warmer, suddenly before we knew anything we have turned into the Mediterranean sea, and the sea life has all change, lots of dolphins swimming in the bows of the ship, riding on the waves as the ship cut through the sea.

* * *

I asked my section chief, "What are we doing here?"

He said there was trouble on one of the islands and we have to help get all the English ex pats of the island. We all had to be issued firearms and live ammunition, I thought to myself it sounds serious this, lots of the lads were quite excited, I couldn't see the fuss myself. Anyway a few days later we arrived offshore of one of the islands and all the liberty boats were sent ashore full of the Royal Marines that we always had on board. I had to help man one of the liberty boats, it was quite cool, the Royal Marines were all fired up over something, we beached and the Marine deployed into the interior of the island. It was about eight in the morning the weather was great, we made several trips back and forwards to the ship, then about 10am we were told to stand down but to stay alert.

I didn't have a clue what for and wondered if I had missed something, as you remember I loved swimming and the sea was just so inviting, I said to the crew chief, "what are we waiting for?"

He said, "the Marines will be back later with lots of civilians."

"When will that be chief?"

"Not till sunset," he replied, "we can go for a swim then".

As I started to strip off, before you could say anything the whole of the beach party was in the sea, next we had volleyball and football going on, the guns were all stacked in a neat pile out of the way, and we were having great fun. As the sun started to go down we could see hundreds of parachutes coming down in the distance.

"Is that our guys chief?" I asked.

"Shit no," he answered in a slight panic, "get you weapons and man the liberty boats."

Just as we were making a dash for all our stuff we could see vehicles coming down the sea road at a great speed, all hell broke loose as we started getting people into our boats and back to the ship, the Royal Marines started to man a perimeter as we could hear the sound of small arms fire, the people we had come to get off the island seemed in a real state of shock, well eventually we got everyone back to our ship.

The next day the captain was telling everyone well done, as he did his rounds on the ship, when he came to our section the

Fleet Master-at-Arms was with him and as they passed, he beckoned me with his finger, I thought I'm for it now, he leant over and with a smile on his face he said, "who won the football then?"

"Why us of course sir."

"Well done," he said quietly with a smile. Only the Royal Navy could have a game of football just as a full-blown war is starting.

Between all the armed forces there is great rivalry and banter, but when the crunch comes, you will always find the British Armed Forces standing shoulder to shoulder. So, over the years there have been many wars and conflicts, and I could tell you in detail about them, except they have all been well documented and you don't need my input, what I think will interest you more is how the beast develops and what are the things I had to deal with personally.

The armed forces are much like any other workplace or industry in as much that, people are encouraged to move towards promotion, well that is fine when you haven't had your whole childhood and young years robed from you as I did. How do I deal with the beast? What are all the issues? How can I being branded as thick, stupid and lazy, ever think I could advance in anything? The impregnation of the beast is something I have to deal with every minute of every hour, and of every day.

I am a young man now, I am in my prime, I should be doing all the things young men in a normal environment would be doing and thinking about, but I am consumed with hate, confused with humanity. I am lost in a world of ignorance due to the messed-up education, or should I say the failure of my school to educate me and give me some basic human rights in our society. Everyone is looking at how they can advance and what extra training they might need, not me I am just looking how to survive and how to keep everyone at a distance without creating a problem. I have really become the master of manipulation, and I am so good at it most people don't even know I am manipulating them or the situation. I have become the master of volunteering, because it always creates brownie points, and as it is virtually impossible for me to pass exams, I need all the brownie points I can get.

The Josh Mann has clicked on to something with me, sorry that's the Fleet Master-at-Arms, to give him his full title, he spoke to me one day and said, "You are a good swimmer, aren't you?"

"Yes sir," I answered, "well we are short of ships divers, why don't you speak with the diving officer, if you become a ships diver you will automatically become a leading seaman."

That's my next inline promotion, I gave it much thought and the first chance I got to speak to the diving officer I told him what the Josh Man had said, to my complete surprise he said, "I know he has already spoken to you about it as he mentioned it to me also."

Well very quickly things were put into motion, the diving officer explained to me that I would need to go back to Sea Shanty to do the formal course and get my qualification, and that I would be able to stay on the ship and on crash and salvage because as a ships diver you still must have your normal ships duties. The diving officer also set me up a training programme on board so that I would know exactly what I would need to do, he even arranged for me to take the written paper on board ship. So how that worked was this, the dive officer gave me some instruction and then asked me the questions on the test paper and he wrote down my answer, but only when I got the correct answer, if I got the question wrong he would keep asking till I gave him the right answer. Needless to say I pasted with 100% and then he sent the result to the diving school, in order to make everything easier, and speed things up. So when I had done enough training with the diving officer, I was fixed a date and flown off the ship to an airfield in Spain and then flown back to the UK by the Royal Air Force.

I passed my diving course and was given my leading airman's rating, when I came back on board ship with my new rating and straight away a posting as a ships diver, there were plenty of raised eyebrows, well the beast and me didn't give it another thought, my new rating gave me a lot of new privileges, like I could boss those people below me about without having to bully them. I now had authority and the beast liked it and he used it very well, my crew chief was pleased as well but he didn't let on.

So the first live dive I had to do was a memorable one, there had been a heavy piece of equipment lost over the side of the ship and it had rested on the seabed, it was about 30 metres down and we had been tasked with recovering it. It was a heavy piece of equipment and we would need to get several lifting strops underneath it to bring it up, the problem was it had embedded itself in the mud, so it would take a very long time, I came up with a plan that if the mechanics could extend the cable on the jumbo then we might be able to get a linkage attached and winch it up with the jumbo Crane. The only other problem was the sharks, I thought to myself what a good way to die, being eaten by sharks. There actually wasn't much chance of that as the sharks were white tip reef sharks and they didn't want us for dinner.

Everything was set in place, it took a while to prepare everything then it was time to start winching, the problem now was trying to get the suction effect from the machinery being stuck in the mud, free and it was clear at that depth the jumbo just wasn't powerful enough. So the next thing was to attach the ships two-inch mooring ropes on it, and get the ship to tow it out of the mud, then the jumbo could do the rest, well nine hours later we had the machinery back on board and all the diving team had lots of brownie points. It was great fun as well, a fantastic experience.

We also managed to do and see lots of things as part of the diving team, as the ship sailed around the world, from the Mediterranean sea, across the Atlantic down by the Gulf of Mexico, back to the Mediterranean, through the Suez Canal into the Indian Ocean, right across the Indian Ocean to

Malaysia, stopping at one of my favourite places, Penang Island, Malaysia, a British colony. Then we would make our way around to the South China Sea, through the Indonesian Islands, and to Japan, Australia and New Zealand. So much to do and see, cultures, wildlife, people, all manner of languages, the realization that we are so small. Many times on my journeys' the beast would be hard to control, because I was with people off the ship that didn't have respect for other people. Yes here you are now, me and the beast talking to you about having respect for other people, you didn't see that one coming did you?

The beast and I found respect in a very strange way, I think because Max and JJ had abused and raped me so bad and caused so much damage, that if I saw it while I was travelling or I would hear stories about it on board ship, then the beast would go into an absolute rage, and usually cause some considerable damage to the offending people. But whenever I was in front of the Captain, the Fleet Master-at-Arms managed to smooth the way, I would sometimes catch myself thinking, I wonder if the Josh Mann has a beast and he really does understand me!

Well now we are informed that the ship is going to make its way back home to the UK, not good for me don't know what will happen. The rumour is that most of the ships company is to be sent off to other drafts, who knows were? Not good I thought to myself, I had to move quickly we only had five weeks before we got home, then almost by magic I got called to the Josh Man's office, quickly I thought I haven't done anything wrong for a long time.

"Morning sir," I bellowed.

"Sit down," he took me by complete surprise, he then spent the next 45 minutes telling me how I could get my next rating up to petty officer, it started with a lecture over the beast and keeping it under control, otherwise the beast would ruin everything, I almost thought that the Josh Mann liked me, but I quickly dismissed that thought. Ok this is the script, because I had done two and a half years at sea I had to spend some time on land, drying out we called it, but if I was clever I could put in for salvage diver, this is the next step up from ships diver, and there are very few written tests, it's all done by what is called manual assessment. I would have to go to the top end of Scotland as soon as we arrive back in the UK for sixteen weeks training, and then the Josh Mann said if I came away as petty officer salvage diver he could get me on his next ship, a brand new troop carrier, *HMS Dark Shadow*. I agreed, and the Josh Mann set it all in motion, I had one drawback, Scotland was the place were Max had started my abuse and rape, when I was only 10 years old, you see you had forgotten that hadn't you? You didn't really want me to remind you. Well sorry and all that but if I must be reminded then so do you.

I went ahead with the plan and I struggled so badly with the beast, we really did not want to go back to Scotland, at one stage I even asked the Josh Mann, if I could do the course in some other place.

"Why?" he asked.

I couldn't tell him, I was so close, in the end I just stumbled out with, "It's such a bloody long way sir". He gave me a really stern look and said, "long way, you have just spent the last two and a half years, travelling all around the world, now stop pulling my chain and get out".

"Yes sir," as I quickly made my retreat.

We arrived back in the UK and I had three weeks home leave, lots of money in my bank, and don't forget the money stashed in my mums loft. I didn't really want to go home, I didn't know what sort of reception I would get, if I got any at all. I had only spoken to my mum about five times since I left home, I travelled all day on the train home, I was in a compartment on my own for most of the journey. I got home and as I walked up the path, I could see the garden was doing really good, lots of roses, one of my sisters had seen me from the upstairs window and started shouting, "Mum, mum it's our Freddie and he is all grown up".

My mum came to the door and as she opened the door the first things I could see was a gang of little kids, Mum with a tear in her eye said, "come in stranger let's have a cup of tea and you can tell us all about it".

We all went in to the parla, I was so very nervous, I thought to myself who are all these little kids, mum looked me right in the eye and as she started wagging her fingers from side to side she said, "no, no they are not mine, they are all your sisters kids".

"Wow," I said, "someone has been busy Mum".

"Yes, it's your four sisters none of them can keep their knickers on or their legs crossed".

There was a scream from the kitchen as one of my sisters gave out at my mum,

"It's the truth," Mum said, then as our cup of tea came Mum asked, "how long are you home for?"

"Just a few days".

She didn't know but all I had come for was my money in the loft.

"I suppose you will want to see Max and JJ."

With a gulp I said, "that would be nice".

Mum then went on to tell me all sorts of stuff that had gone on, the one good thing was that Max had been moved to London as his mum and dad where not well, and that JJ was living in America. She did say that she got more cards from them than she did from me, I think I was supposed to be feeling guilty or something, but I hadn't forgotten how they had all got rid of my Dad.

"I don't know where you are going to sleep," mum said, "I will have to put some cushions on the floor or you can sleep on the sofa down here".

I said to mum, "the sofa would be fine."

Well the evening was a little chaotic with everyone trying to introduce the new tribe of kids, the noise was horrendous, and I could not wait for everyone to go to bed, in the middle of the night, I was in the loft got my money and was gone, I was so amazed it was still just where I had stashed it. In the morning I walked into the city and as I was having a breakfast at five in the morning I was feeling a little guilty about how I left Mum. I just could not stay in that house, to many bad memories, the beast was well pleased, and if he could come out and give me a pat on the back I am positive that he would have. I left Mum a little note and some money in an envelope, I did tell her to use the money on herself, but I am positive she wouldn't.

What to do know? I have got nineteen days leave and a pocket full of money, my travel warrant will take me to northeast Scotland, so I can get a train that goes up the east coast and stop off along the way.

* * *

I have got off the train in one off the north east cities, they speak real funny and the city is just like any other city in the UK I guess. People in poverty, it is a seaport just like where I grew up and the dockyard is just the same, I could be at home, so apart from the fact I haven't got a clue what people are saying, it is really familiar, the pubs are the same, all along the dock Road and on almost on every corner. The ladies of the night are out, even in the daytime just as at home, I really don't know why or how we came to call prostitutes ladies of the night? I have got myself booked into a B&B for a week, it's a sleazy place, well that is what my Mum would call it, to me and the beast it just seems like home. It is so good not having to wait for someone to get out of my bed before I can get in, I think people have found out I have plenty of money, as I seem to have a lot of friends all of a sudden. The beast is enjoying the girls, and he is having a feast, for me I am still lost within myself, what the hell am I? Who on earth am I supposed to be? Are there any real people, other than the ones I can buy, bully or use?

The days just flew with ease into the nights, I was getting lazy I hadn't trained for more than a week now, I decided to go for a run along the Dock Road, it must have been about ten

miles long, so that should have been a good work out. On my
run I had a good heart to heart with the beast, and told him
we cannot go on in this way, whilst he is enjoying himself I am
getting lazy and unfit, as I pass a buttie van and a couple of
young girls serving gave me a wolf whistle and a big smile.
That's new I thought to myself, "why ye a canny fit lad," one
shouted, I think it was a compliment, on the way back I had to
stop and ask for a drink of water, the girl that had shouted
after me said, "why I' it will cost ye like".

I had to push down on the beast, and told him this one is
different, this one is mine, "how much?" I replied, as she gave
me the water she leaned over and nearly come clean out of
the van.

"It'll cost ye a kiss now and the rest on tick till the night."

"Ok," as I grabbed her and nearly pulled her the rest of the
way out of the van,.

"Why, steady on tiger," she said re-composing herself, "We
will see ye at the Red Lion at eight o'clock the-night".

"Ok," as I started off back up the road, the beast was
giving me a hard time, he wants to do her good and proper,
but something is different, this one is not the same.

Evening time came and the Red Lion was the pub just along
from where I was staying, I got there early and was having a
game of darts when she walked in, the beast was jumping out
of his box, "no" I said to the beast this one is mine. There
were two men in the window seat near to the door, and they
seemed very familiar with her, the red mist started to stir,
"what are you doing?" I said to the beast. "This one is mine,"

Then the barman said to her, "your usual Jenny?"

"Yes, Mark thanks, and a pint of beer for my new friend
here," as she walked towards me and the beast, she was
stunning and different to all the others. She came over to me
she said, "Ye will-ne be needing those darts tonight I have got
plans for you sailor".

Ok that's it, that's as much as you get to find out now, I told
you all she was different. The night went well and the rest of

the week flew by and as I continued my journey to the northeast, I could not get Jenny out of my mind, she was the first women I have not had to buy, and it took a lot keeping the beast under control. Jenny and I agreed to write to each other and we had our photo taken in a camera shop, and for many years she was to become a big part of my life.

So, my Journey continued to *HMS High Lander*, and my advanced diving course to become a salvage diver. When I arrived I had a message to see the senior dive instructor, I thought to myself, I haven't done anything and I am in trouble, it was an instant reaction in me that if I was summoned to see anyone my first thought was I would be in trouble of some form or other. It was the way as a youngster that I processed everything, I never had good news ever, so it was natural for me to have a first response or reaction to something negative.

To my surprise this time it was good news, I was called into see the senior dive instructor who was also the section chief, he said to me, "I have two reports here, one from the dive officer on your last ship and a more interesting one from the Fleet Master-at-Arms on your last ship".

"Yes chief," he went on to say, "The dive officer said you have a fearless attitude to diving and that it needs to be kept under control".

"Yes chief."

"The report from the Fleet Master-at-Arms is more interesting, he states you are a very complex person, who responds best to firm and strong leadership, but that you need to be given more than normal leeway with regard to the academic side of instruction".

"Yes chief."

"So what does that mean for you and how does it affect your learning?"

"Chief, I don't read and write very well, my reading is very slow."

"Ok," he said we can deal with that, I like to get everything out in the open before we start.

So then the chief gave me an intro pack, and said I had better get a head start on the other trainees, and read the pack tonight. I noticed that everything in this camp seemed very laid back; people on the camp were going around in tracksuits, not uniforms. I was shown to my quarters and I had my own room, it was amazing, the petty officer who was showing me around, said, "There is no ceremony here everyone is just the same as the next guy".

"Why have I got my own room?"

"Everyone has their own room, there is a lot to learn and you have to do a lot of personal study".

He then showed me around the rest of the camp, it was amazing, I got back to my room and got stuck right into my study notes, I need to be in class room number one at 10.00hrs in the morning. My cover notes gave me a heart murmur, it seemed a lot of work, I didn't mind the work, it was just if being thick, stupid, and lazy could hack it?

As I got settled in and opened my notes the first page read like this.

~ Dive physics and decompression chamber operations.
~ Operation of a remotely operated vehicle (ROV).
~ Underwater demolition.
~ Topside and underwater welding.
~ Hazchem / nuclear diving.
~ Offshore survival and safety.
~ Deep sea diving techniques and procedures.

All the above wrapped up into, Inland diving, Offshore diving and deep-sea diving. To say I had gone into a cold sweat doesn't even begin to cover how I felt, even the beast has a shake going on, I opened the next page and it was headed up what to expect on day one. I must admit that by the time I had got through it I was feeling a little better, and my problem wasn't that I could not remember things, it was that it took me so long to read it.

The next morning I went for breakfast as I got into the mess hall there were people sitting down with waiters serving them, as I turned around to walk out thinking I had got the wrong place, I had a gentle tug back on my arm and a gentle little sweet voice said, "Sir might I have your name?"

I answered, "Yes, my name is Mak'a".

"Yes, I have you on this table," she showed me to a table that had a few men already sitting and eating, she then having sat me down started introducing everyone to me. I was so confused, I was being treated like an officer, I was positive I had gone into the wrong building, and we all looked the same in the same track suits. The beast is telling me you had better find your way out of here, and take that good looking girl with you. I was ok once I had sat down, because remember JJ had sent me to school to learn silver service, so I at least knew my table manners.

It turned out that this was the norm, when we finish the course we will be Petty Officer First Class, one of the instructors came and sat at the end of our table and introduced himself, as Tiny, he said everything was very informal and relaxed, we would get to know everyone on first name or nickname terms. For some reason I decided I would use the nick name *The Beast*. It seemed most people used nicknames; I appeared to be the only one who had the brief prior to our introduction to the course and staff that happened right after breakfast. Tiny turned out to be my personal instructor and my dive buddy, the reason I got the course work 24 hours before anyone else was because I was so slow at reading, and when I took exams, my dive buddy Tiny was allowed to read the exam papers to me. It was absolutely amazing, the course was a lot to take in but no one was in a rush, Tiny said this sort of work is about taking your time doing all your safety checks and then doing them again, what we called by the numbers. There wasn't much classwork and academic work, most of the work was practical and physical. It proved to be an amazing time, and the beast never made a single appearance, I was quite surprised, but then again the whole course was done in such a relaxed and friendly atmosphere, don't get me wrong it was a very demanding course, there was no drinking allowed and we was a very tight unit. The senior dive officer was a commander but everyone called him the bomb or bomber because when he dived he could sink so fast, no one could keep up with him.

* * *

You will be pleased to know I passed out with flying colours, everyone did, and I am now a Petty Officer First Class and I am on my way to my new ship, *HMS Dark Shadow*, as the ships salvage diver. In my new post, I would now oversee the diving section on board the ship. I was happy and anxious at the same time, I had written to Jenny and gave her all my news or as much as I was allowed to say, and let her know how she could reply back to me on my new ship. As soon as I had reached *HMS Dark Shadow*, I was instructed to report to the Fleet Master-at-Arms, he was so pleased to see me and was proud I had passed my course, "You will be wanting to see your new quarters then".

"Yes sir."

"You will be bunking in with my number two here, Petty Officer Stanly," he then called Stanly in his office and introduced us both, "Take him away Stanly," he growled as if to say the niceties are over now back to normal. Stanly showed me to our cabin, what is this? I thought, a cabin and not a mess hall. We shared the cabin with two other Petty Officers. The next few weeks were very busy getting everything ready to sail, my department was once again a very small unit, five other divers and me. The other men were just ships' divers not salvage divers and they all had other jobs on the ship, the only other salvage diver on the unit was my station officer, Lieutenant Patrick (Pat) Mendelson.

He was my boss and officer in charge, he seemed ok, but it wasn't until we were at sea I started to get to know him, he wanted everything on first name terms whilst we were at sea and on our dive unit. At the end of it all if there were anything important to do, deep-sea or armament, then it would be him and me, and we had to be able to rely on each other totally, so rank had to go out of the window. Every opportunity we could get to do a practice dive we took it, we had to keep up on the time we were actually in the water, each one of us had our diving logs and our dive time was recorded in dive minutes. Every now and then we would be out in the middle of the world's oceans – on war exercises usually with the Americans or Australians – the object would be to detect and destroy, obviously just by way of an exercise, and this would give us the opportunity to use mine detection tactics, it was all good fun. One year we were called into action for real, at times it was quite nerve racking, we had practiced for years and now we are doing it for real, every time the ships alarms sounded my heart would stop a beat as we rushed to action stations, and had to put on our gear that protected us from bomb flashes and fire. Sometimes we had to be at action stations for days, as soon as we put on our gear, the adrenalin would start pumping. We would be part of a battle group, and we experienced our share of live action, our ship was also used as a hospital ship, not something I would want to expand on, you understand.

* * *

The years rolled by and I worked my way up to Chief Petty Officer, and ended up as an aircrew diver and winch man, working in an air sea rescue team, we saw several live actions and wars, and on the good side travelled all around the world several times, I saw many beautiful places and met lots of wonderful and extraordinary people, memories that will remain with me forever, the beast stayed with me and was never detected, but many times I was told I was crazy, usually for the risks I would take, but that side of me was the beast.

For a few years I got an attachment to the Royal Marines parachute regiment, I only took it because I wanted to learn how to jump out of airplanes and at the time there was some great training available. The regiment I went into were looking for experienced divers, some of the training was done in the jungles of Borneo and along the Amazon, it was challenging work but fantastic. Eventually we got used to the mosquitoes or maybe it was the other way around, whenever we were with tribal people they would laugh and say the mosquitoes love white man, we thought it was funny to, it must just be the new blood!

I got to dive in some extraordinary places because I had to be allowed to keep up my dive log, I had a wonderful time learning how to cave dive in some extreme places, the guys I was with had a wonderful time to because everywhere we went I was the nominated cook. I got quite adventurous and even sometimes exotic, with king snake and alligator kababs and freshly picked herbal salad straight from the jungle. Lots of great fresh fish to BBQ and in Asia the famous fish head soup with lots of spices, and much, much more.

On one of my trips back to the UK – or I should say home – although the beast and me now regarded the world as our home, I never had anything to relate to my natural family about, my early years were terrifying memories and still haunt me to this day. I found it difficult to relate to the western world as the civilized world, because I had found more humanity in the jungle tribes around the world, progress always linked arms with greed, inhumanity and war! Well here I am now back in England, not happy to be home if I can call it that, waiting for orders. I was summoned by some very senior Navy and Marine officers, and given the following brief.

In one of our home Police Forces there is large scale corruption, I was to go in undercover and join the Police Force in question. I would be fast tracked and join the Police underwater search team, this unit would be called out only when required, and I would assist with regular training or practice dives, my normal police duties would be with a CID unit and this is where the corruption was believed to be.

This all sounded a little strange and I wasn't very happy with it, but at the end of the day orders are orders. I was given two weeks to be fully prepared for the operation, then I went to a Police training camp in the south for 12 weeks. I hated every minute of it, me and the beast got in quite a lot of trouble during the training and at one stage were threatened with being thrown out. A Royal Marine intelligence officer came to see me one weekend, just before my final exams, because as you know I was not an academic, I was told the only person that knew who I really was was the Chief Constable of the force I would be allocated to in the north, and that when I took the exams just do my best. I told him there would be no way I could pass these exams, he confidently informed me that I would pass with flying colours, I knew this would not go down well with the men in my recruitment, so I just did what I was told.

The day came for the results and you would never guess I not only passed but I was top of class, this also gave me an award, the other men were not happy, the passing out parade came with lots of family and friends, except for me. I had tried to get in touch with Jenny but we had not kept up our contact, my fault as you might guess. The Royal Marines sent me a sister I never knew I had. 'Rebecca.' she was to be my contact on the ground and would feed any information back to HQ, she was really nice and we got on very well right from the start, the rest is left to your imagination. I will help you a little, we got very close over the next few years, and she seemed to understand about the beast, although we never spoke about how he got there, she just stated I should get my temper under control, she never knew what you know, that I am bad-tempered, stupid, thick and lazy.

I was sent directly onto the underwater search unit, we would have our training days most Fridays, we spent the day in some nice location diving in rivers, or reservoirs, then about mid-afternoon on our way back we would manage a pub crawl, it didn't matter if we all got drunk, because we were the national police underwater team. All our vehicles were marked *Police* and we had emergency lights and sirens, attached, no one in those days would interfere with us. Part of the crew we had were two regional crime squad officers, and they would work between both of the units, from time to time I knew some things that would be going on that were not quite above board. The crime squad officers would meet with undercover drugs officers, it didn't take me long to win their confidence and be included in some of the things they would be getting up to. I was mostly used as a driver of the *Jiminy* speedboat, this was a rapid response boat that was on its own trailer unit and was fully equipped, with everything that would be needed to effect water board search and rescue. The unit was pulled by a long wheel based, state of the art, Range Rover. This vehicle was also fully equipped with tactical support equipment, such as body armour, ballistic shields and small arms firearms, we could be deployed at a moment's notice to anywhere in the UK, but our base was in the Midlands area. The sort of everyday things we would be called to do would be searching rivers for contraband that may have been dumped as a result of crime, missing persons in lakes, ponds and rivers and then there were the thing we would do as result of our own enquiries. I was quickly accepted for several reasons; I was single with no obvious family members except my made up sister Rebeca, I was a very accomplished diver, I was a rapid response police driver, I could handle myself, firearms trained, as far as they would know do as I was told and keep my mouth shut, all in all on the face of it one of the lads!

Over the next few years I would be part of a network of crooked police officer, that were in it for their own gain, very cleaver, always did enough for the big bosses to think we were doing an excellent job, I even picked up a few Chief Constable's commendations. So what sort of things did I get evidence of? Police corruption on a huge scale, fabrication of evidence to gain convictions on otherwise innocent people, convictions of drug smuggling, but not of their own set up, big ringers with a network of stolen vehicles. All these things were up and down the length and breadth of the country, involving many police forces, I was very useful because what they thought was my temper was actually the beast. I could fly off the handle at people and these guys would encourage it, I was amassing a mountain of evidence and I kept it well undercover and safe because these guys thought I was a loner, well they were right, the only person I had in my life was the beast. Whilst on this national unit we lived very well, but not so well as to attract attention, I am positive there were some very senior officers involved but I could never get solid evidence against them. We had a great record for finding drugs just offshore around the coast, well yes we did, but we always knew it would be there and only a small amount that we brought in would be handed in, and we never quite managed to catch the people responsible. Once in a while the dealers at the top of the chain would surrender someone they wanted to get rid of out of their own organization, usually a North African in the country illegally and with no understanding of English.

So it came to a time that I had to make all the evidence available for prosecution, it was a massive job and to be honest not one I was looking forward to, I was very nervous and for me that was unusual, the armed forces secret service gave me a few of their people to help me put the case together, and all this time I was still active with the guys I had been spying on. The only way you could leave this outfit was in a pine box, then came the time for the arrests in all 22 people were arrested in four different locations throughout the country, it had to be well organized and executed by the military secret service, in order that they didn't get tipped off, and obviously, I had to be arrested also. It was tough going because none of the arresting teams were told I was on the inside, so I got a good kicking, the beast put up a good fight and everything looked good as I was arrested at the bosses house. He kept shouting at me to calm down but I think with all the adrenalin going on I could not get the beast under control.

I ended up in hospital with a concussion and several broken ribs, this ended up being a fortunate advantage, because I could be identified by the chief constable I was working for and taken out of the picture. The gang would not know what had happened to me as they were all separated and held in lots of different places, it would be fourteen months latter everything would come to a massive Crown Court presentation lasting seven weeks. I was never identified and gave my evidence behind blackout screens, and my voice was electronically distorted so they could not identify me. I thought this was a little crazy, because I was the only one not in the dock, so it didn't take them long to find out it was me giving all the evidence, they were all convicted and sent to prison, they were sentenced to 330 years between them at an average of fifteen years each. A great result that made me somewhat a hero in the eyes of the armed forces, but what was to become of me now? I had been doing this job for more than four years, Rebeca and me never made it, she saw too much of the beast and ended up quite afraid of me.

After it was all over I was given three months leave and an option to either return to the Royal Marines or stay in the Police Force, the Chief Constable I had worked for was very keen for me to stay on and even offered me a promotion, I had been earning a lot of money, I was paid a police officer's salary and a retainer by the Royal Marines, and now I had to choose to go back to one wage, or I could just leave both jobs with a very nice bonus?

I decided to stay in the Police Force with the assurances from the Chief Constable that no one would be able to find out who I was and what I had been doing. I was asked what section of policing I liked the most, and I let them know I would like to be a police dog handler, there was strict criteria for becoming a dog handler, and all handlers were married men, so I was put on a training course in a part of the country I had not worked. I bought a house with a large back garden, it was a lovely house four-bedroomed detached house with large gardens on the edge of a golf course, it was a few miles from the dog training centre. This centre was run by civilians and not police officers, and I was told there would be no back door in. If I was going to be a dog handler then I had to do it on my own merits, that was fine for me as most of the course was practical learning, and if I could achieve this on my own merit I would be working by myself, just me and the dog.

I was accepted on the training course was accepted and I was the first single man to start the course, I had to have my house inspected the first week to have it passed as ok for the dog I would eventually be trained with, and I passed with flying colours. So, as I started the course I was told that very often the dogs pass the course and the handlers don't, that we are marked separately, I was given a lovely jet-black German shepherd dog, and I called him Guinness. He was eighteen months old and was already a very big dog with a great big character, we didn't start too well as Guinness was a handful, he was ok but at the start I was failing him, one of the instructors called me into the office and gave me a formal warning. We was about half way through the course, so I was very bold and said, "look I really want to pass more than anything I had ever done in my life, and if there is something I am not getting right it is not that I am not trying".

He went on to say he and the other instructors could see how much I wanted this to work and that I had built a great bond with Guinness, but that we were coming to the part of the course where we get to take the dogs home. So I got very bold again and said, "look if I am doing well and Guinness is doing well but there is something that I am not getting, then it's not that I am not getting it, it's that you're not explaining it".

He conceded that I might be right, so he made me an offer, that as I lived so close to the training camp why didn't I come and help at the weekend with the staff and may be get some hints from them, I jumped at his offer and in the first weekend I worked out what the problem was.

As I would send Guinness into an aggressive attitude I was getting all worked up as well, it was almost impossible for me to stay calm, the beast was getting in the way, and it was making me look more aggressive than Guinness, I made an agreement with the beast that he would take a rest while I get through the course and then once I had passed and we had Guinness home the beast could come back out. I had made lots of improvements by working the weekends looking after the kennels, and scored some extra points with the instructors, it has always been the way with me, I might have my failings, I might be bad tempered, thick, stupid and lazy according to my branding, the part that is definitely not true is lazy, I have been and always will be a hard worker!

The training with Guinness was going so well now and the bond between Guinness and me was growing at a rapid rate, Guinness was a very clever dog and he totally trusted me his obedience to my commands were so sharply, the whole school was noticing the way we worked together, One of the tests was to see if I could get Guinness over a very high wall on the obstacle course, Guinness loved the obstacle course and the wall was no problem to him, one day the senior course instructor came and said, "You see the height of this wall".

"Yes sir," I replied.

"This is the height to get you both through the course."

"Yes?" I replied inquisitively.

"We are going to put the wall another twelve inches higher to the course record, how do you feel about that?"

"If twelve inches is the course record then you had better put another six inches on top of the record because Guinness will smash it and he will go anywhere I send him without a second thought."

"Ok then let's see what he can do".

The wall was made of horizontal planks of wood six inches deep, the instructor asked if we wanted to try the record height first?

"No sir lets set it as we agreed," I insisted.

I gave Guinness about ten minutes warming up on the obstacle course first and as we came to the wall each time I let him see the wall but called him around it, Then when his muscles were nice and warm I didn't take him around the course I took him with a good run up, straight at the wall, as Guinness hit the wall I gave him the command over. He scrambled a little and I nearly jumped in to help him, but I managed to hold back and went around the wall and called him from the other side, as he got his front paws over the top I could hear his back legs working like crazy to get himself over. As he got his front shoulders and his head on the top of the wall, he paused and looked at me as if to say what is all the fuss about as I called him over. Guinness and I rolled about fighting with his favourite reward toy, then, all the instructors came over shouting and saying, "well done – well done."

It was a wonderful day and I was so proud of Guinness, that weekend was the first weekend I could take Guinness home, we had such great fun that weekend and our bonding was complete.

The rest of the course was just a formality and when we had our passing out ceremony everyone except me was surprised to see the Chief Constable wish us well and give us our badge of office and swearing in of the dogs It was a great day and I knew the Chief Constable was there for me. The instructors stated afterwards at the celebration buffet that that was the first time the Chief Constable had attended any of those occasions. All the other handlers and dogs families were there and I said to the senior trainer, "well that's a lot of firsts for this recruitment don't you think?"

"How is that?" he replied.

"The first time you have had a single guy on the course, the first dog to set a new record on the wall and the first time the Chief Constable attended," he gave a smile in acknowledgement.

My first day on the job as Police dog handler arrived, for the first month I had to be escorted around by a more experienced dog man, we mostly get used when on our week of nights. During the day we attend some schools as part of a team showing what the different parts of the police do, Putting the dogs through regular training, keeping them happy and keen. Guinness is an absolute dream and we are inseparable, there has been lots of talk on the division about the guy's that got sent to prison, and I just had to abstain from all the talk.

Guinness and me soon got a reputation for being the number one team, at any incidents where I had to use Guinness as a tracker, he would always find who we would be looking for, and in disarming people with weapons he was fearless; just like me. It seemed to take the edge off the beast, except if anyone tried to have a go at Guinness there would be big trouble. One time four guys thought it was funny to make Guinness angry while he was locked in the van and I was in a shop on enquiries, I could hear Guinness while I was in the shop taking a statement, I knew he was ok but the beast got very angry. I suspended the interview I was taking and went out of the shop, four guys were banging on the van and shouting at Guinness, as I walked towards them I said nothing, they backed off right away and as I got to the van I just said you like to play with dogs do you? I had a long staff in the back of the van and took it out by this time the four men could see what I was going to do, and started to run along the road, they very stupidly jumped a fence and ran into a small wood to hide. I put Guinness on his long lead, he was ready for business, I took him over the fence and into the wood, then made a radio call to the control room to state I was in pursuit of four men on foot for suspected criminal damage and gave my location. By the time reinforcements arrived Guinness had a taste of all four men, and my long staff had a few dents in it, we never found the men, but we did get a message that four men had attended the local hospital with nasty dog bites. The station Sergeant asked if I would like to go and identify the men, I just said I didn't get a look at them.

He said, "I hope they don't make a formal complaint".

I just smiled and said, "Somehow I don't think so," and that was the end of that, Guinness and the beast had quite a lot of fun that day. Guinness got to know the beast quite well and they both worked well together on many occasions, one time two men jumped off the roof of a factory they were robing just to get away from Guinness and the beast, both ended up in hospital with broken legs, another time a man ran into a police station to seek refuge, from Guinness and the beast, we had pretty much a free rain all over our patch, and we got quite a reputation for getting the job done. Don't get me wrong, if people we were after didn't try to run then there was no need for Guinness and the beast to get involved other than to contain the situation till help arrived, except on one very well-known occasion when we had cornered a man for molestation and rape of young boys.

The crime squad had set up a sting operation but it went wrong and we were called to help look for the man. I am being polite calling him a man, we caught up with him in a known location for these people, and he immediately gave himself up as soon as he saw me and Guinness. In the back of the van, which is set up with two cages in the event that I have to transport a second dog, so I put this animal in the van next to Guinness, and I intended on calling it in to control. Guinness was going craze in the back of the van, and the man was screaming his heart out, it was such a commotion. There was no way Guinness could get to the man and the man was perfectly safe, well I never did make the call, and somehow we strayed a little off the beaten track. I stopped the van on the edge of some farmland on the edge of the city, and told the man he could go free, I told him that if he went across the field it was the shortest way to safety, he had gotten about fifty yards away and I could feel the beast very unhappy, I reasoned with the beast and said if he goes to court nothing will happen and the boys he had abused and raped would have to go through hell in the process. It reminded me that Max and JJ had never had to stand in judgement for what they had done to me, and then the red mist descended down. It was a full moon and a very quiet evening, then Guinness was away followed at speed by the beast, the red mist stayed for about three and a half minutes, and when it lifted I was cleaning down the back of the van, Guinness and the beast. When I went on duty the next day I was informed by the Duty Sergeant that the man we had been looking for had been found and was in a critical condition in hospital, and he asked if I knew anything about it. I just said probably the fathers of the boys he had raped must have found him, I never gave it a second thought and as I left the station to put Guinness in the van I think even the beast had a satisfying smile inside him.

So many years pass by and so quickly, Guinness and I have managed to obtain three Chief Constable's commendations, and Guinness is coming to the end of his working days, Police dogs only work actively for seven years, then they can retire, and as Guinness' handler I get to keep him, as it came up to that time I was asked if I wanted a new dog, and then Guinness could work part time, I declined and opted to leave the police force altogether, it was also around that time that the police officers I had put in prison were due to be released, and I knew they would come looking for me, so the decision was made we would both leave. I put my house on the market and as soon as it was sold we moved right down to the south coast. There was no fuss when we left the police force, none of the usual leaving parties, Guinness, the beast and me were loners. The only thing that happened was I got to meet the Chief Constable for his own personal thank you, I appreciated that.

CHAPTER SEVEN

The Pub Years

I had an overwhelming urge to own a pub, so ended up working as trainee manager for a big company, Grand Metro Ltd, I got through the training in eighteen months, the different training pubs I went to, I was always allowed to take Guinness with me or I would not have gone, Guinness always came in handy at closing times, and now and again when people got out of hand, he never had to be in attack mode his bark was enough to make people desist no matter how drunk they were, there was a very sobering effect in Guinness, as I was sent out by the company as a fully-fledged landlord, we quickly got a reputation for cleaning up wild public houses, and Guinness and the beast loved it, I was able to command from the company very big financial bonuses, eventually we had saved up quite a large amount of money and I decided it was time for us to have our own free house pub, it didn't take long to find it, a nice country pub with a big front and back garden, and a sizable car park, we set together a three year plan to build the pub to its maximum, I called it the Drunken Sailor.

The first year was settling in, getting the restaurant built as an extension on the side of the pub, the second year was consolidating what we had, and then the third year was to maximize the potential, it all went near enough to plan. Guinness and I had many ladies following us, for Guinness it was easy, for me as you could imagine not so easy. We had done really well and got the business to where we wanted it to be by the end of the third year, we had some good times and some not so good times, mostly because of the beast. I found out that if I drank too much alcohol then I had less control over the beast, we got away by the skin of our teeth a few times, and were reported to the police on one occasion. Three young gay guys had come in – not regulars just passing through – and they were not happy with the frosty welcome from the beast. It was very difficult, one of them said he was going through a sex change after I challenged him for using the ladies toilet, so I ask him if he still had his pianos and balls, he answered me yes, so I said to him he is obviously not a women then, and gave him a warning about using the ladies. He never heeded my warning, so he had to deal with the beast. It wasn't pleasant and his two friends tried to help him and Guinness dealt with them, the local Police Sergeant was a regular at the pub so there complaint didn't go so far, but a few days later the Sergeant did give me an unofficial warning. There were no further incidents of that kind and the business was doing well.

About a year later everything had been going ok but Guinness became very unwell, he had a tumour, the vet said that because of his age it would be best to put him down, I pondered for a long time with what to do, and Guinness started to suffer more so he was put to sleep. I suffered so much after losing Guinness and it brought back all the pain as a boy when my dad died, at least I was able to say goodbye this time, but it would be a long time before I would be ok again.

My heart had gone out of the business, and people were getting more of the beast than me, so the takings were steadily going down, I made my mind up to sell everything and move away. It didn't take long to sell as it was a good business, a man and wife with two young children, had inherited some money and they were the ones that took the business over.

I didn't know what to do and had no plans, so for a while I was just drifting around, I had sold everything I had and was travelling very light, in the evening wherever I ended up I would slowly stand in a pub until closing time, and end up being put out onto the street, usually after an argument with the beast. Several times I ended up in police cells for the night to sober up, and then let go in the morning. One summer's morning I ended up on a park bench in a small village, the village was in Norfolk, a very flat part of England known for its quaint villages and network of rivers, where the local people would harvest reeds, that would be used for thatched roofing. The village was called Waverly, and at each end it had a pub, the pub at the north end of the village was called the Waverly Inn and the one at the south of the village was called the Waverly Way, I thought this was strange yet very quaint, the local people nicknamed the two pubs North and South, the North I noticed was up for sale, and had a temporary manager in it, and the South was owned by a widowed lady called, Bella. I stayed in the village for a short while as it had a nice feel to it, the park bench had a roof to it, and Bella would allow me in the mornings to use her flat to shower once I had sorted out her cellar and cleaned it all up ready for the new days business.

Bella had a very special way about her, she was loved by all her locals, and in the village it was by far the most popular pub, for some reason when I was in Bella's pub the beast was not around, in fact he never made an appearance the whole time I was in that village. It was as if the place had a spell on it, yes Bella's spell. I got less and less drunk, and was known by people as Freddie the keeper of the park, I had started to put lots of flower beds all around the village and several people had offered me a room, but I declined, I got used to the park bench, and I had a key to Bella's back gate so I could keep my bags in a safe place, nobody seemed to mind me being there, in fact it was the total opposite they liked me being there.

I started helping old people with their shopping, I even did a little work for the local farmer, but people were perplexed as to why I would insist on sleeping on the bench, I got to confide with Bella quite a bit but I never told her about the beast, and she had a very calming effect on the whole village, I had told her about my time in my own pub, and about Guinness, she said to me, "why don't you take the North it's been up for sale for a long time?"

I don't know what it was about Bella but everything she said made sense, and I had started to drink a lot less, she was the first person in my life I could talk to, in fact the village was full of lovely people and a very calming place to stay.

I took Bella's advice and bought the North to everyone's amazement, I had only spoken to Bella about it and had put it to her that we would be in opposition for the same customers, and she said I was no match for her because her customers were regular and loyal, she was absolutely right.

By now I had stopped drinking almost completely, and the beast it seemed had been put into retirement, I was struggling with the North because Bella had all the trade, but I was for the first time in my life at peace and around good people who I could trust. I would only speak at any length to Bella, and people in the village knew it, they tried very hard to get information about me from Bella, but it seemed that as soon as I had Bella's approval then I had everyone else's. To one side of the village at the start of the lane leading to the next village there was a little old church, and at times it was almost hounding me even just to stand and look at. I had been asked by many villages to go to church, it seemed every Sunday morning just about everyone would go to church, including Bella. People soon learnt that I didn't do church and they should not ask why, on Sunday mornings I would clean all the pipes for my pub and then go and do Bella's, and I was left alone over the subject of if there is a God or not, everyone knew I was firmly in the 'is not camp'.

Time moved on and my little pub started to do ok, I think it was more of Bella's doing than mine, I noticed that from time to time that people would divert from the nearest trunk road, into the village for food on their journeys, so I decided to convert my pub into a small restaurant and B&B. I got permission from the local authorities and put up large signposts on the main roads, it took only three months for all the work to be done, and we became very busy in a short period of time. All the business in the village were happy as it brought a lot more people through the village, I really began to think that life could become worth living at last, nobody had seen the beast for two and a half years. This had become a very calm period in my life, people in the village began to hear wedding bells around Bella and me, but all the bells were in their heads and wishful thinking, neither Bella or I had any intention of getting married, although we could often be found in the mornings coming from each other's establishment.

It was not long before the wheels started to fall off, Bella became ill and was diagnosed with breast cancer, she became very ill and so I decided to sell the B&B and move in with Bella to could help her keep the pub going and recover without the pressure of the pub, the only way she would accept this was if we became partners so the deal was done.

Bella got through the first attack of cancer and seemed to recover well, she had lots of support from the village, but just when we thought everything was ok the cancer came back, only this time it seemed worse. So now we had another spell of about eighteen months of treatment, operations and sickness, most people know what this all entails. Bella was amazing even in her worst state she would put on her wig, make herself presentable and come into the pub to see all her friends and public. Things were now starting to get back to normal, me and the beast became very protective of the Bella, and just being in her presence seemed to have a calming effect on everyone, the beast has been quiet now for some time, and on a few occasions when Bella and me were on our own I came very close to telling her that I loved her. The beast always managed to talk me out of it, saying that I would not know what love was if it slapped me in the face, and I suppose he is right, I have never known love so how did I think I could be in love with anyone, but I did get a sense that Bella knew something?

Life had just got back to normal and Bella and I were talking of going on a holiday, I have never been on a holiday with anyone, since Max took me when I was ten and the abuse and rape started, remember that was when the beast was sown inside me!

Bella and I have been getting very close to each other and one night just as we were finished in the bar, we had planned to relax, with some food, a bottle of wine and a movie. I was getting the food ready, the bottle of wine was nicely chilling and the movie was ready for me to push play, Bella was just having a shower and getting her PJ's on. I was thinking that tonight I am going to tell Bella that I love her, we have just two holiday places left to pick from and then in the morning I will make the bookings, the beast is telling me to wait until we are on holiday, but I think I am ready now?

All of a sudden from the bedroom Bella lets out an almighty chilling scream from the bedroom, I quickly turned off the cooker and ran in to see to her, she was collapsed on the floor sobbing uncontrollably.

"Bella, Bella, whatever is wrong?"

I picked her up put her onto the bed and repeatedly asked her what was wrong, eventually, her wailing reduced to a sob, she was still unable to speak and she took my hand and placed it under her left armpit. As I gently manipulated my fingers, there it was a small lump, about the size of a pee, Bella was under strict instructions from the hospital that if she found any lumps, no matter how small, she was to go straight to the hospital. I helped her to get dressed, phoned a taxi and we were in the hospital in less than thirty minutes, Bella for all the wrong reasons was well known at the hospital, and she was seen to right away, she was admitted and a multitude of tests were done, by 4am the verdict was confirmed the cancer was back and Bella was going to be kept in hospital. I made all the arrangements for the pub as I didn't want to leave Bella for one moment, over the next three weeks the cancer got worse and worse, and eventually very suddenly one night the cancer took her life. I was devastated beyond belief, I did get to tell Bella that I loved her, but by the time I told her she was already in a coma and I doubt she ever knew just how I felt. My emotions were all over the place, the beast was now putting in an appearance almost every hour and then it suddenly dawned on me I had Bella's funeral to arrange.

Back at the pub the news was out and everything from that moment seemed to be in a very strange mist, I had started to drink almost all day, the staff at the pub and some of Bella's close friends seemed to take over, I could not speak to anyone about anything. I had people telling me this and that, but nothing was sinking in, I was beside myself with grief, then out of the blue on the third morning after Bella had passed, just as I was opening the pub, a man and a young lad appeared insisting on speaking with me. They came into the pub and he announced to me that he was Bella's husband and that the boy was her 17-year-old son, and they had come to take over all the arrangements for her funeral.

Now hang on just one moment I was thinking, now I know there is no God, as my head began to go into a swirl and the red mist started to fall the beast was fully awakened, the first thing that went was a bar stool, the beast flung it almost the full length of the bar, then the man instructed his 17-year-old son to wait in the car, a good move on his part and as his words seem to be none stop.

"I will also be selling the pub, because it belongs to me," then my head began this enormous pain, the guy just would not stop talking and kept spouting his demands, "I need to have a calm discussion with you about when you are going to leave?"

I don't think my head can take any more pressure, the beast throws another stool and then me and the beast grab this guy and almost without his feet touching the floor through him out of the door, as I growled to the staff, "everyone takes the day off, the pub is staying closed today." As I was locking the door the guy is shouting that the police are on their way. Without a word the beast has knocked him clean out one punch, just like in the old days. I went in the pub and locked up, then put all Bella's favourite tunes on the juke box, and proceeded to get drunk just me and the beast. Well we had quite a party it lasted three days and nights before the police eventually broke the doors down and carted me off to the police station, sort of semi-conscious, I was eventually sobered up by the police, served notices by a solicitor and told I could not go back to the pub, my personal belongings had been packed for me and left in the police station. There was a letter the solicitor wanted me to sign, for me to give up all my rights to the pub, well he got told were to go very politely by the beast, the police said that under the circumstances there would be no charges, but I could not go back to the pub. I really didn't know what was going on, I was so confused and went and booked into a bed and breakfast in the next village.

I could not go back to the pub, and I was banned from going to Bella's funeral, apparently the beast had done such a good job none of the villagers or so called friends wanted anything to do with me, and especially the beast. Nothing would make any sense at all and how could Bella have a husband and a son and not tell me, and what of the so-called friends in the pub? Someone must have known Bella was married, by now I was drinking far too much and by the end of each day it was all I could do to find my bed at night, I was barred from every pub in three villages, and I only had two days left at the B&B, the beast was on duty every day and in fact all people would see was the beast.

Bella's funeral went on without me and eventually Bella's husband was able to close the pub and sell it off, to be fair to him he did make me a payment for my share of the pub and he was not stingy. So now it was time to sober up, lock the beast away for a few days and move on, my life became like a mist travelling from one town to the next, drinking far too much and letting the beast out on many occasions. The winters were very cold and the summers very wet as I recall. I had got myself a pushbike and a small trailer on the back to put my things in. I had a small one-man tent, and we got along the road as far as we could until I was so drunk I could not sit on the bike any longer. Many nights I could not even put my tent up and just rolled myself up in it, in my drunkenness I was robed many times, but a few times the people who tried to rob me met the beast, and we ended up robing them. Life now was just an empty space, nothing and nobody, just me the beast and the road. One night – I don't even know where we were – me and the beast were staying in an underpass on a busy road, because the rain was like a tropical monsoon, I think somewhere between Newcastle and Hull, me and the beast took a really good kicking. We tried to fight them off and before I passed out I remember the beast doing really well, but there were just too many of them, me and the beast ended up in a hospital. When we came around I recall it was very bright and my head was pounding, I don't know if that was from the kicking or the hangover, all that we had left was the few ragged clothes in the locker at the side of the bed. Apparently we had been there for three days and the police interviewed us to see if we could remember what had happened, but it was all a bit pointless, we were in the hospital for another ten days and the doctor warned us about the drinking and how if we didn't stop the alcohol would kill us both.

The hospital had put us in contact with a charity that might help us get back on our feet, and two weeks without a drink had given me and the beast time to reflect on what we would do next. Our time came to leave the hospital, the charity had given us some new clothes, well not new, hand me downs like when I was a kid. The lady from the charity came to see us on my last morning in the hospital and tried to help us further, but me and the beast were unanimous, we didn't need any help thank you, so we are off on the road again. I asked the beast were we should head for this time, I fancied Hove on the south coast, I remember it being nice there by the sea, and I was still feeling a little delicate, but the beast was full on and ready to go.

"let's go to the nearest pub, get drunk, and then head for London."

The beast won and I don't remember much of the next few days on our way south to London. Working our way south through every village and town, pub by pub, we somehow made it on to a motorway services and crashed out on a bench. When we woke up it was starting to get busy, a nice guy who was a trucker sat down near us having a full English breakfast, I said to the beast, "when was the last time we had proper food."

"I don't know he replied."

The trucker asked where we were headed; I think by the state of us he could see we had no form of transport.

"We are on our way to London, pub by pub".

He laughed in a wonderful way and said, "who are we, are you travelling with someone?"

I replied to him, "When I say we I mean me and my conscience".

The tucker went on and stated that, "If you and your conscience have got time to get a quick shower in the gent's toilet while I finish my breakfast, I will give you a lift to London as I am going that way."

As I got up the beast said, "What do you need a shower for, when you come out that guy will be gone".

I showered anyway and when we came out the trucker was waiting for us. We had a good chat on the road to London and true to his word the trucker dropped us at the big market place in the city centre, which is where he was making his delivery. We thanked him and went on our way, it was still very early and right away the beast noticed that the market pub was open for the traders, we went in and ordered a pint of beer. The lady behind the bar said you can only have beer at this time if you order food with it, I thought to myself this is a bit strange, and the beast said we was being conned, so we ordered beef burger and chips, the beef burger for me and the chips for the beast. We sat there until we overstayed our welcome, that usually meant we were drunk, so we found a nice park, the sun was out and we had a few hours' sleep on the park bench.

We were nice and peaceful, when all of a sudden we were being shaken, I thought London was in the middle of an earthquake, but no it was two coppers, (police officers) shaking us and saying, "come on now you cannot sleep there," we knew that story so I just replied.

"Ok we are on our way," we wandered around for a while and stumbled upon a night shelter, I was still sober enough to make enquiries as to how we could get a bed for the night, a man on the door said you come back between seven and nine pm and its first come first served until we are full. He went on to say the place will probably be full by half past seven so come early. Well it was three or four nights before we would be sober enough to get a place in the night shelter, and each morning after breakfast you get put out and then each night it is first come first served. So over the next few weeks we never made it there very often. When we did make it to the night shelter and were allowed in, it was very well organized I must say. I was fed hot evening meal and English breakfast. I was given a single room, was able to do my laundry and have a shower.

There was a quiet room where there were people to help and talk with you, then a games room with a pool table, and then a TV room with nice cosy chairs. The people giving the advice told me how I could go to the housing and the benefit office to maybe get help with money. I went one morning as we came out of the night shelter, direct to the housing and benefit office, while we were sober. I had a ticket and I queued, nearly all day, when I had my final interview the lady told me I didn't score enough points to go on the emergency housing list as I was classed as fit and well, not in any immediate danger. I was not a vulnerable adult and had no dependent children.

"So what do I do now I asked?"

She stated that she could give me a note for the night shelter that would give me priority to get a bed each night, that she would put me on the normal housing list and when I had worked my way to the top off that list, I would be made an offer of accommodation.

I asked her, "How long do I stay in the night shelter for, she stated that it could be as long as eighteen months to two years. I was flabbergasted, in the cubicle next to the one I was being seen in, was a Somalian family, the mother and father and five children between the ages of 11 years and three years, I remember feeling sorry for them as we had spoken to each other in the morning because they had queued at the same time as me, and I wondered how they would cope on the street. I had worked and paid taxes all my life and I could not get any help whatsoever, so what would they do? When I was finished I waited for the family, to offer them what help I could, we still had some money in the bank, the beast said it was a bad idea, let's just go to the pub, I must admit we had been in those offices all day and it was getting on for five pm. We decided to wait and see the family because it would not be long as the offices closed at five pm, just as we were making up our mind, they came out of the office very joyful. I asked the man "how did you get on?"

'Fantastic," he replied, speaking in good English, I was baffled because in the council office he had used an interpreter, "we have been given an emergency payment of £1,500 for clothing, they have booked us all into a family room in a hotel with meal vouchers for the hotel, and told us we now have a permanent case worker to help us until they find us a permanent home". To say you could push me down with a feather was an understatement. Here's me an ex-soldier and police officer and I don't even score a point on their system, I think something is very wrong!

Back in the pub after a few pints me and the beast felt very aggrieved and everyone that looked or sounded like an immigrant became the target of our abuse and anger. It wasn't a good situation and the beast was well ready for anything, the whole day just enraged us both, the more we drank and the more we reflected on the injustice of government policies, the beast was getting really out of control. We got thrown out of every pub we went to, and lost count how many times we got warned by the police for our behaviour. We went to the night shelter; it must have been well after 11pm and got warned by the night manager that they would call the police if we didn't go away. We managed to get a bottle of rum just before closing time and ended up by the river, drowning our pain, the beast had started to calm down and I was feeling very sleepy. I didn't remember the next few days, it was just a blur, it could even have been a week or more, we never made it back to the night shelter, and I was ready to die. I had – had enough.

I now took charge of the beast for the very first time, we are going out of the city I told him we are not drinking anymore and we are going to find somewhere nice we can just curl up and die. I said to the beast it will be ok, it won't be painful and it won't take long, the beast was stunned, and I was very clear on what I had to do. We got on the road to the south coast, it felt very calm and we managed to get to Brighton just in two lifts. I don't remember any of the conversation with the drivers that had given us the lifts to Brighton; there was just a very calm sense of emptiness. The beast tried very hard to get me to go to the pub and get drunk, but I was in control, we wandered up and down the south coast for days, not eating and then only drinking water, I seemed to be almost in a trance and the beast could do nothing. I would find myself often reflecting on what life would have been like if my dad had not died, and Max and JJ had not got hold of me, so they could repeatedly rape me for all those six years of my young little life, or what if I had been strong and brave enough to tell someone. When I thought about it in this way, I felt quite sad and all that I had to show for it was a life of continual pain and the beast, so now I have made up my mind to kill the beast, I must die!

I had lost count how many days and nights I had walked up and down the sea front, I was by now very weak and nearly ready, I had seen many years ago, how aborigines could will themselves to a permanent sleep and then just slip away and die. The beast was almost silent by now, but like me he had no strength, we just kept going from one bench to the next, and every night I would expect it to be my last night. When I woke up in the morning I was shocked to see another day, a sip of water and move to the next bench, night time would come and then another morning. Then just as I was getting myself ready to sleep and thinking to myself this is it my last night, two men came and sat down beside me, normally if anyone did that they would be off because of the smell.

I smelt of the death I knew it was coming, but for some reason these men didn't move and when they spoke to me it was so calm and peaceful, I thought this was how I was going to be taken, one of the men said where would you like to go to? I don't care, anywhere, it won't matter.

Then he said but it does and said it with great authority. "Why does it matter to me, you can smell the death on me".

The second man who also spoke with authority in his words said, "We can take you to a place where you can rest and be looked after, and the glory of God is all around, otherwise the place where you are looking to go, you can never return from."

In my mind, I was furious at the mention of a God, with my best energy I replied to the man, "There is no God so don't talk as if there is".

Then the first man said, "There is a God, but you have chosen to reject God all your life! You are making a choice now, we want to help you make a better-informed choice".

At this point I was really wanting the beast to make an appearance, but he was totally silent, almost as if he was not there at all, it was so strange I had never been without the beast. I could not find him, the two men were not going away and they just kept on about this place they could take me too where I could be looked after. In the absence of the beast I had to make a decision all on my own, were can he be? I was too week to argue any longer so I conceded, they took me a short distance to a nice car, one of the men got a flask out of a basket and gave me a nice cup of hot sweet tea, it was so good. The other man got in the driver's seat and we were on our way, to where I did not know and didn't care, the tea was so nice.

Before I could ask any more questions I was being woken up from a deep sleep, and I was so at peace with everything, the man that was driving said with a smile, "Our guest is awake, we are almost there".

It was morning time and I could recognize we were somewhere in the Cotswold's, a beautiful part of the English countryside, then before long we pulled up a drive banked on both sides with flowers.

"Where am I?" I asked.

"This place is a Christian retreat centre, you will be safe here."

We pulled on to a car park at the back of some lovely old building's, a huge garden was off to one side, and beyond that a stream and more fields, I was beckoned out of the car and walked around the buildings into a courtyard with masses of flowers everywhere, and an ornamental fish pond in the middle, full of Chinese coy carp. I was taken into a big dining room, there was a lady in the kitchen preparing some food. It smelt really good. There were tables laid out for about 100 people, "Who lives hear I asked?"

Another lady appeared from behind me and said with a soft voice, we have a community of people here that come for all sorts of reasons, we are a Christian community and we look after people of any and all faiths and of none.

I replied in an uneasy voice, "Well I am the none, there is no God I can promise you!"

She went on to say, "That is fine that you think that way and nobody will try to convince you otherwise, but we all believe there is a God and that Jesus Christ died on the cross to save us all from our sins!"

I now started to feel very nervous and I wondered again where the beast had gone. They offered me some food and I accepted it gladly; it was delicious, a very tasty beef broth. Somehow my thoughts of dying had completely gone, the two men that had brought me to this place I never saw again and I could never find out who they were. This place was so calm, if I believed there could be a heaven then I guess this could be it. After my broth I went for a good walk, this place was amazing and it was a working farm. Right at the top of all the fields I found some big barns there, and a couple of men moving bales of hay. They stopped for a while and had a chat, one of them called Edward said he was one of the community elders and that he was in charge of the working part of the farm, and he told me a little about what they do, day to day.

It sounded really cool, and everywhere was so peaceful, lots of cows, sheep, a few goats and pigs, and some well-kept beehives. After my walk I went back to the farm buildings, there were many old but well-kept buildings, the main building was a huge barn, looking magnificent and to one side of the courtyard, the door was open and I could hear music and singing. I walked in and apart from the musicians and singers, there were two elderly people, a man and a women sitting in great big armchairs, as soon as they saw me they got up and introduce themselves and at the same time the old man waved his hand kindly at the musicians and they stopped practicing so we could talk without shouting. The man said in a very soft and reassuring voice, "Hi you must be our visitor from Brighton, I am Roy and this is my dear wife June, come and sit with us for a while".

They ushered me to a sofa and I sat down, then without prompting the musicians and singers left and as if by magic a young lady brought a tray with tea and biscuits. Roy said in a very proud voice, "Welcome to the Open House of Jesus! This is a place where people from all kinds of backgrounds and faiths can come without any fear without any prejudice and for any reason, they stay with us of their own free will, for a few days, weeks, or months, and some never leave, we work the farm to enable the community to be self-sufficient, some people come as paying guests on retreats, others don't pay but work on the farm or in the community serving our paying guests. There are no phones, radios or TV's, no newspapers or magazines, and no smoking or drinking of alcohol".

I thought to myself this sounds a cool place, then Roy said, "We would be happy for you to stay a while if you would like to? You don't have to make up your mind now, stay a few days and see how you feel, I am sure you could do with the rest, and if you have any question just speak with anyone, or come back to me and June."

"I think that would be great," I replied, because I had a good feeling about the place, I was a little concerned about the beast!

A guy about my age came and showed me to a room that was in a converted stable. It had a single bed and its own bathroom at the side; it was decorated really nice, in keeping with the whole place. He said his name was Billy, and that he was always about if I needed anything or just wanted a chat, we became great friends So now you can guess that I stayed a while, six months to be exact, and in that time the beast made quite a few appearances, but nothing too extreme, just enough to let me know he was there. It was a truly wonderful place, but I never did find out who the two men were that took me there. I never turned fully to God, although Roy did give it a good try, June said the two men were probably angels sent by Jesus, and that that had happened before. It was so sweet of her, but I don't think so. God had never done anything for me so why should he start now? I still had the beast, Roy did at one time say a very profound think that has always stuck with me, he said, "Freddie we never lose our demons, we only learn how to live above them!"

I often wondered if this was what he meant about me and the beast? The farm was a magical place all sorts of wounded people, being put back together by love, there was lots of unconditional love, wherever that came from I don't know but it was there. I had only seen this type of love once before and that was with Bella, it is quite strange that the times when I experience this love the beast never shows up! I learnt many things in my six months, it was a beautiful summer. I learnt many things to do with farming, from rearing the animals and taking them to the local slaughterhouse, then butchering the meat and making it ready for the table, how to know when is the best time to take in the harvest, and the part I really enjoyed was learning how to be a beekeeper and extracting the honey.

Such a great experience, then on a personal level, learning how to be humble and kind when there is no reward for it, I got this to a certain level, but the one I refused to give any attention to is forgiveness. No matter how hard Roy, June and the community tried, I was never going to let it go, I hated my family for never letting me say goodbye to my Dad, I hated Max and JJ for their years of abuse and rape, and I hated myself for letting it happen and being complicit to it, and I hated having the beast inside me. Roy knew there was some deep and painful anger inside me although I never let on what it was. I was so ashamed of it, and I owned it now, it was all mine! During the six months, I had many internal battles going on especially with the beast and I felt as if I had gone as far as I could go, so after some reflection and in agreement with Roy and June it was agreed it was time for me to move on.

I didn't have a plan and Roy gave me a little bit of money and said the door was always open for me to return, any time I wanted to. So me and the beast set off for the North East of England I don't know why, it always held some hidden attraction for me, it wasn't long before a familiar pattern started to re-emerge, we got drunk and the beast came out, and then we were on the fringe of society again, in spite of the six months on the farm, something had to change and I knew it was me that had to do it. I had to take control of my life and the beast and I knew the only way I was going to do that was to stop drinking and stop the beast, I remembered what Roy had told me and I kept repeating it to the beast, I am above you, I have the control, and I had to convince myself of that also, I stayed off the booze for two weeks and I started to get myself in a more physical state of fitness, when I had left the farm I was in good shape mentally and physically so I had to first get back to that, I did it and I kept the beast under control.

CHAPTER EIGHT

Work Hard and Play Hard

Suddenly a good job opportunity came along with a bullion security firm, I went for several interview's and I was taken on as a customer service manager, because of my military and police experience. I had a lot of on the job training that meant me travelling all over the UK as it was a national company and the company liked the fact that I was single. I ended up looking after areas where permanent managers were either off sick or on holiday, it was a very good job and it kept me very busy, I had completely stopped drinking and the beast had been kept under me for a long time, but was definitely still there, I was on the move a lot and it was great for me because I was staying most of the time in hotels and the money was very good because I got all my expenses paid, then after about three years, I was offered a promotion, to look after the whole of Greater London area.

I was not sure at first and asked for time to think about it, then one of the company directors took me to one side and said, "look Freddie it is like this, plain and simple, today is Thursday 1pm I need you in London by 8am on Monday it is the highest paid job for someone at your level in the whole company, there are massive bonuses to be achieved and people in the company have been fighting for this job for years. This offer is never going to come your way again, you will jump in one leap to being the highest paid customer service manager in the whole UK, so I don't have the time or the will to let you think about it, I am going for lunch and I will be back in my office at 2pm, I want my secretary to inform me when I return that you are on your way to London OK!"

I think you can guess that I gave his secretary the answer he wanted before he had even got out of the building. I went to London and threw myself straight into the job. I was totally focused for three years and was earning an amazing amount of money with hardly any time to spend it, my bank balance was very fat, I had a well sought after postcode (W1) and I lived across the road from the famous Hyde Park. I was a big success for the company and myself, the beast had been kept under control, I hadn't had an alcoholic drink for many years, my friends who I only saw on a limited occasions were senior bankers, directors, stockbrokers and millionaires, and they would often tell me they could make me lots of money with the right investments.

I kept my hard earned money in the bank and had a rule with myself it was staying were it was, they could never understand why I was single and would always be trying to fix me up, usually with someone else's wife, that used to infuriate me, and on a few occasions it would irritate me to the point where I would let them have a brief look at the beast. One of them even commented at a party that there was something very dark about me, and that he didn't want to investigate it. They all knew I was an ex services man and they always put it down to something that happened in battle, so I was happy to let them think that. I didn't fool myself that they would be real friends, but at times some of them could be good company, my work was going very well although it was very demanding and took up most of my time, there was no such thing for me as normal time or overtime, it was all the same, I worked however many hours I needed to get the job done,

To make certain I qualified for my bonuses, which got paid every six months, I never missed one target in three years and life was good, there just had to be a THEN! I bet you could see it coming, well here it is, I met a wealthy man who was a retired banker and investor, he said that if I would trust him with some money he could over a period of time get me a massive return on my money, far more than I could imagine. I had got to know the man a little, had been to his home and had dinner with his family. Well the deal was this, I would give him the cash no questions asked, and in one year he would give me back the cash three times over, less his commission. The problem of being in one of the financial hubs of the world is your reality gets twisted, and once you start getting a lot of money you get greedy. I had done really well at work, but to keep it up I could never take proper time off or holidays abroad, and the way this man groomed me was with all the things I had not yet done, yes I went for it. I gave him a lot of money almost all that I had saved, the year went by and then came the time for my return, you guessed it, there was NO RETURN and after a little pushing and shoving on the missed deadline and promise after another, I had to swallow my pride and accept that I was not going to get any of my money back not a single penny. I had still not been drinking and the beast had been locked away for so long, the beast was now screaming at me to go and sort the guy out saying he has lived long enough anyway, I looked at taking him to court to get my money back, and I went to see a solicitor, who basically said if the guy didn't give the money back then I had no case to take to court, he offered to write to the guy just to see if he would admit having being given the money; that failed with the guy denying everything. So that was that £150,000 down the drain, I pondered for about three months what I could do, he had completely shut the door on me and I could see him laughing on the other side of it, the beast was relentless at me it was now effecting my work and for the first time I missed my bonus target.

The beast kept telling me to get drunk and go and do him in; I knew whatever happened I could not get drunk. Then one night I was trying to occupy my mind at home with some clearing out, seeing what I had that I could sell, I came across an old gun I had acquired as a souvenir, and then I found the bullets. I loaded the gun and sat looking at it on my kitchen table, with the beast bellowing in my ears, go on what are you waiting for, my head was ringing and as much as the beast was saying go and do it, something in me was saying get rid of the gun. I think the gun sat on the table for three days and nights, then my rationale in my mind said this, I served my Queen and country and was asked to kill bad people or people we were told were bad, then I was a police officer that if it had been required of me could have been called to kill bad people, so now I can do this for myself, and that was it.

So me the beast and the gun went to give this guy one last chance to give me my money back, It was about 7pm and I walked up his drive and knocked the door, his wife answered the door but didn't open it, she just spoke through the door. I thought this was strange and she repeatedly insisted that he was not in, I knew of a few places that he might be, so I went looking for him, the last place was a mutual friend, who's house we would go to and play cards, Benny. He was a bit of a recluse and an eccentric, he always enjoyed us going around but would never go out, I knocked his door he lived in a block of flats on the first floor, when I knocked on his door he said right away, "Freddie you look really terrible come in whatever is wrong". I was in a daze Benny took me into his living room and gave me a shot of his best malt whisky, it hit my brain like a thunderbolt, and I quickly asked for another then another, I started telling Benny the whole horrid story, he was beside himself and kept telling me that there must be some mistake. Just then there was a massive bang and we could hear the front door getting smashed in, as we both jumped up, three police officers presented themselves in the living room doorway behind a shield that filled the whole of the doorway. One of the officers was shouting for us both to lie down on the floor, Benny jumped in front of me and started to protest, I knew how bad this was going to get and I pushed Benny out of the way and onto the floor, then presented the police officers with my gun. They quickly retreated shouting into their radio "firearm, firearm," it had all happened it a flash of time.

Benny and me sat down again and started to have another whisky, the front door was completely flattened, I said to Benny you better go out this is going to get very messy, the beast was so excited and doing summersaults in my head, Benny refused to go saying this is my home. I told him we have got about ten minutes before the firearms response officers come, please go now, as he was again refusing to leave me the telephone rang, I answered it and had an initial conversation with a detective inspector who said he was now in charge of this situation and he asked to speak to Benny, when Benny got on the phone he was furious and really gave the Inspector what for and piece of his mind, so now the armed response officers arrived and we were all at a standoff

The police started to evacuate people from the building, using a rear fire escape that was just out of my line of sight. My head was spinning and the beast was in overdrive, and I could not get Benny to leave, the beast kept on at me lets shoot it out, the police kept wanting to speak with me on the phone to keep me occupied and insisted that Benny was being kept by me against his will. I somehow got through to Benny that he wasn't helping me by staying and after about two hours he finally left the flat in one piece. For me it was a different matter, the picture was getting very messy, I kept on thinking who did the police speak to and what story were they get told to make such a forced and rapid entry into the flat. I was still drinking Benny's whisky and I knew it was not helping. The beast was nonstop in my head and the whisky was making the beast more excited and giving him more power, I kept saying the words Roy had left me with, that we live above our demons, but this time it was not working, I knew my job was gone, I knew I would be going to prison, and prison as an ex-police officer did not look appealing right now. If I started more of a commotion the likelihood is I will get shot dead by the armed police officers that by now would be all around the flat covering every window and possible exit point as I am only on the first floor and could jump out of one of the windows.

I went to the front door or should I say the opening where the front door was, as soon as I showed myself, I could see two armed officers on the half landing going up the stairs, stooping behind a ballistic shield, and an officer on the ground floor near to the door but tucked underneath the concrete stairs going up. On the other side from that officer was a half flight of stairs leading to Benny's flat, the officers were screaming at me to put down my gun and step out of the flat. I said nothing and went back in, by now they had got a professional negotiator and he tried hard to keep me on the phone, and he was getting on my nerves and between him and the beast I was finding it very hard to think.

I told the negotiator I would not speak to him anymore because he was irritating me, so after a while longer he got a women to speak with me, I was very surprised that by now they had not rushed me in order to overpower me, that seemed strange. I had made my mind up that I would present myself at the door and force the police to shoot me dead, suicide by cops we called it when I was a police officer, and that would finally get rid of the beast. Obviously the beast was not so happy with that idea, but out of everything in my life I wanted to get rid of the beast, I drank a few more whiskies and came out of the door and stood facing down the stairs. I had my gun in an offensive stance, pointing right at the officer in the lobby, I was surprised that the officers from upstairs didn't right away come running down, and I was expecting there to be lots of noise, it was a very calm moment, and only the officer in the lobby spoke, he was instructing me to put down my gun, and to lie face down on the floor,.

I shouted down to him, "do you know who I am?"

He answered, "Yes".

"Then you will know my military record and my police record."

"Yes."

"Then you will also know with this G104.5 semi-automatic hand pistol I can shoot straight between the concrete stairs at your head and kill you outright, and that I have far more combat training than any of you," and I aimed my gun right at the point where I had said I would fire, I felt now in total control except for the fact that the officer didn't know I had no intention of firing at him and I was only trying to provoke one of them to shoot me dead. The officer then panicked and presented himself directly at me, on the flight of stairs, I could see that he had an MP5 semi-automatic rifle, and I saw the muzzle flash as he fired his weapon.

In an instant, out of sheer recall reaction I fired one shot directly at his chest, the officer had already turned sideways ready to run out of the door behind him. As my bullet hit his armoured jacket it went in sideways on and catapulted the officer out of the door. I never felt anything from his bullets and then in a millisecond there were at least three officers jumped on me from behind and overpowered me. I passed out and woke up some time later in a police cell, when I woke up I was so angry that I was alive. I was restrained face down on a mat with my hand and legs secured behind me, as I turned my head I could see two armed officers in each corner of the cell, one shouted out to the sergeant "he is awake".

I was in pain just about all over my body; the sergeant came and instructed the officers to take off the restraints, and warned me that if there was the slightest movement towards any one of them, then the shackles would go back on. I didn't reply, I was so confused if I was going to wake up then why was I not in hospital, as the shackles were taken off the officers retreated out of the cell door, and the sergeant stated a doctor would be along shortly to see me, as the door was closed I noticed that all my clothes had been taken away and I was in a paper jump suit. I checked myself all over I was covered in lumps and bumps, so many bruises all over me but no bullet holes. I know the officer that had fired at me got off a bust of fire that would be between three and five rounds. He was only nine feet away from me but not a mark on me, I could not accept that he had missed, he could not miss at that range.

I was seen by the doctor and everything had gone calm, I was three days in the police cells being regularly interviewed, I just gave my story as I knew it to be, I went to magistrate's court and many charges were put before me and the case was referred to the crown court, I was remanded to HMP Blaketown on old London Victorian prison.

I was so angered I was not dead, and I was not feeling well at all when I was in the court room, I was put in a van on my own and transported, to the prison, the process in the prison was formality and I could feel myself slipping away, I could see and hear everything that was going on but for some reason I could not respond, it was like I was there but I was not there, a total numbness come over me, I was seen by two doctors who were trying to get me to respond but I just could not, I was put in the prison hospital and I remember just going asleep, and I stayed asleep for the next fifty-seven days.

CHAPTER NINE

Blackout

This is how it was for the next fifty-seven days, I was in a single sell in what the prison calls strip conditions, this means the suit I am wearing is made in such a way that it cannot be torn or cut, it is very heavy so there is no need of bedding there is a sink and toilet made of stainless steel and with rounded edges so there is nothing sharp I can use as an instrument to hurt myself. The door was open steel bars so that the officer on the other side could see everything I was doing, and the officers had to watch me 24/7 and make notes every 15 minutes, I was totally numb and only responded when I was told to by the officer the other side of the bars. For example if I was given food or a drink I would not eat until the officer told me to, "drink you tea now Freddie," I would do so, "eat your dinner now Freddie," I would do so, I was totally non responsive for 57 days, as I woke up I kept a diary and this is how it reads.

HM Prison, Blaketown.

No light, no pain, no senses, no vision and no love.

Friday – some awareness some emotion because I have just had a row, 57 days of nothing, no light, no sense, no vision, and no love.

Saturday – No sleep, is it day or night? I am aware of people the other side of the bars, no light, no pain, no vision, and no love.

Sunday – the days and nights just go into one; they slide by, no light, no pain, no vision, and no love, still in darkness nothing inside.

Monday– taken to court, kept in boxes all day, no light, no pain, no space, no vision, and no love.

Tuesday – normal day still in darkness, and no love.

Wednesday – normal day, no love.

Thursday – normal day, no problems, no love.

Friday – cleaning with Alf, still in darkness, no pain, no vision, and no love, feeling low.

Saturday – a bit indifferent day called G, no answer, no pain no love.

Sunday – normal day, no sleep, no love.

Monday – bad day in pain, darkness, no sleep, no love.

Tuesday – normal day, no love.

Wednesday – being moved to HMP Westwood, still in darkness, pain getting worse, no sleep, and no love.

Thursday – normal day, didn't move, still in darkness, fear now, pain and no love.

Friday – been in boxes again all day, now in HMP Westwood, lots of pain, still in darkness, no sleep, no vision, and no love.

Saturday – no sleep, bigger cell, in darkness, asked to use the phone but request refused, getting angry, no love.

Sunday – still no sleep, darkness getting worse don't know if I will survive, feeling very high, much, much pain, fear, very suicidal, phone call refused, never out of cell, cell closing in very small, no air no space, blackness no love insight.

Monday – still no phone call, went to the gym this might keep me alive, still no love.

Tuesday – given up on phone call, starting to get very smelly. I have been refused a shower, very low might give up tonight, no love.

Wednesday – never out of my cell, no sleep, darkness all around, evil, pain and fear, no love.

Thursday – still no shower, banged up all the time, anxiety about the darkness, why go on, no love.

Friday – I had an hour's exercise in the yard round and round still in darkness, giving up now nothing to live for, no love.

Saturday – saw a doctor for about one minute, total waste of time, even more darkness, anger, fear, shame, pain and no love.

Sunday – Final letters to everyone I know, apologizing for my failure and asking their forgiveness, no sleep, phone call request refused, banged up, no hope, only pain and no love.

Monday – very tired, got to the phone today and spoke to an answer machine, where has everyone gone, what happened to love, why all this pain and darkness.

Tuesday– still in darkness and still in bed.

Wednesday – moved to the block, don't think the darkness could get any worse. (the block is solitary confinement).

I have been 24 days in the block, have made friends with all the cockroaches, some of them even have names, last night something very strange happened, the cockroaches never turned up.

Thursday – through the night, I fell off to sleep and at some time in the night, one of the screws, (prison officer) woken me by shining in my face a massive bright white light, as I felt him sit down at the end of the bed, at first I was angry but I could not move, none of my muscles would work, he spoke very kindly, and my anger subsided, there was no sign of the beast, the voice behind the light kept re-shoring me everything would be ok, his voice gave me a profound sense of peace in my heart, as he continued speaking re-assuring words I just fell back asleep.

Friday – at lights out as my cell was in total darkness I instantly thought was I dreaming what has happened, again no cockroaches came out and there was a profound sense of peace in my heart, I fell asleep and again woken with the screw shining this bright white light in my face, the same reassuring voice speaking to me until I fell back to sleep.

Saturday – I had the same screw come into my cell again, and once again none of the cockroaches, the light is so blinding, but he would not turn it off, as I drifted back to sleep I had the most peaceful sleep.

Sunday morning – I asked the screws to stop coming in my cell with that bright light.

The officer answered and said, "no one is allowed in your cell at night."

Three consecutive nights I have been woken up by this bright light, I had amazing dreams, no cockroaches and a profound sense of peace, I was asked if I would like to go to the chapel after breakfast, something in me just immediately said yes, so I was allowed a shower and some clean clothes and four officers escorted me to the chapel. I was sat at the back with two officers either side of me, there was an overwhelming peace all around, I didn't follow any of the service, it was as if I was in my own little world and atmosphere, at the end of the service I was escorted back to the block, and I felt as if I was in a different world.

Monday – this morning I have been moved to the general population and a nicer cell, I was allowed a shower and a phone call, I spoke to a human being, it made me feel good, later two ladies came to my cell door they looked like angels,

Angel – "Would you like to do an Alpha Course?"

Me – "Will it get me out of this cell?"

Angel – "Yes every Tuesday night for one and a half hours for twelve weeks."

Tuesday evening at seven thirty the angels came back and took me to the chapel, I was shocked that I had no escorting officers, just my two angels, as I entered the chapel I felt that same presence, the leader, Rev Tim, said it is the presence of God and the Holy Spirit.

I asked Tim about the light in the cell, he said it must have been a messenger from God.

For the next twelve weeks Tim and his angels lead me on an amazing walk with Jesus from death, pain, emptiness, and darkness into a wonderful relationship with God, in faith, peace, hope and LOVE. Amen.

I finally found Love!

CHAPTER TEN

How The Prison System Works

I want to give you some information about how the British prison system works and as I go through my new life in prison when I share some of the amazing real-life miracles that happened you will understand things a little easier.

The progress through prison is meant to be one of rehabilitation and one of the ways of measuring this is in prison categories:

A. class prisons housing very serious offender's including murderers.
B. class prisons housing medium level prisoners, some may be long term, and remand prisoners, or people who have not yet been found guilty or sentenced.
C. class, known as less serious offences, what is known as paper crimes such as minor fraud, and prisoners working their way through the system who may have been already in prison for many years, working their way to parole.
D. class prisoners, usually in the last twelve months of their sentence, these prisons are designed to gradually re-familiarize people with society and may be allowed out of prison on day release and are encouraged to find work, looked after by the probation service.

So, I am now in HMP Blaketown (B) class prison on remand and waiting to go for trial, I have given myself to follow Jesus

Christ of Nazareth, and I am in the devil's domain, I am a firm believer that the devil has much of the control in prisons, this prison has a high potential to erupt at any time, and had I not found God the beast would have had a field day.

The beast as you will have noticed has not been showing his face, the reason for this, is that the beast is in my head, and my head since coming into prison has been completely closed to the world, and to the beast. I believe that God closed my mind in order to keep me alive, so to do that He had to completely close my mind to shut down all my senses, so that my mind and body could be repaired. Then He came and visited me in order to reopen my mind and senses; that was done by way of the angel that came to my cell on those three single nights, with the brilliant white light. When I was in the block, remember the very first thing that happened was no cockroaches came out, then when the angel spoke it was with a soft reassuring voice that everything will be OK. And the angel kept repeating this message until I fell asleep, it was not a two-way conversation there was no need for me to speak, and the atmosphere in this darkest deepest Victorian dungeon where the devil and cockroaches hang out, was an atmosphere of pure LOVE. I didn't recognize this at the time, but I know it for a fact now.

Then the next amazing thing that happened was my move from the block to general population and my introduction to Rev Tim and the Alpha Course. The Alpha Course is a safe environment to ask any questions you want, and to be able to discuss in a positive way the Bible, God and His son Jesus, all questions are allowed, and the teaching of the Bible is relevant today.

Another thing about prison I need you to understand is the regime of the prison officers, when they come to open a cell door; there are certain rules or protocols they have to observe. That means the status given to any given prisoner, for example if a prisoner is deemed to be unpredictable or dangerous then the protocol might state that when the door is opened the officer opening the cell door, (the turn key) must be accompanied by three other officers, this would be known as the turn-key plus three, or perhaps a six man unlock, the worst I got treated to was, a six man unlock with a dog, it looks like this:

1. The turn-key
2. Four officers
3. A dog handler and his dog.

I will be telling you how I got to that later, most of the time officers are not restricted when opening cell doors, these circumstances are exceptional, except at night when there is only one turn-key for the whole prison, since at night the whole prison is in lockdown.

Lots of things have changed now, my normal day looks like this: 7.30am the cell door is unlocked and I can go down the landing with everyone on my wing to collect my breakfast then return to my cell to eat it. In this prison there are no mess halls, all meals are eaten in your cell, when I get back to the cell I am locked in. If things are good on the wing, about 10am I am allowed out of my cell for one hour with everyone else on the exercise yard. This is just a big yard where inmates if they wish can walk around – in one direction only for some reason. it's always clockwise – during this time you get to talk to other prisoners, or they can talk to you, not always a good thing, it's also a time when prisoners take the opportunity to settle differences'. If that happens lots of officers come from all over the prison to stop whatever it is that is going on, then the wing gets put on lockdown, could be for several days. Lockdown means we are only allowed out of our cell to collect our meals.

The people fighting are taken to the block, and put on charges relevant to whatever has happened, but to start with everyone is punished on the lockdown. These types of disturbances can often be very serious and will nearly always involve some sort of homemade weapon, a chivvy or some form of knife, or perhaps a club with nails sticking out of it, or a razor blade melted into the end of a plastic toothbrush. Well supposing all has gone well, we are banged up at 11am and let out for lunch at 1pm, in the afternoon we are let out at 2pm–4pm for association.

This is when all the cell doors on the wing are opened at the same time, so within the confines of the wing prisoners can associate with each other as they see fit. Not always a good time, it is when the deals are made between the prisoners for different types of contraband, and also when the bullies are active, this is a time when you have to stand your ground, especially for me as an ex police officer. Then at 5pm for dinner; on my wing at this time there are two gangs, the wing is split into four levels, the ground where all the best single cells are, the pantry where food is served, the TV room, and the showers. It is made up of the prisoners who work on the serveries giving out the food, and are classed by the screws as reliable, it is also a job they get paid for, £5 per week paid into their canteen account, they also get any leftovers at the end of meal time, by the way the food in general is quite good, the first landing on this wing is prisoners who may for different reasons be vulnerable, because this level is on the same landing as the office, there is a small secure area for the screws to see what is going on. The second landing is run by one gang of about four prisoners, and the third landing or top landing by another more brutal gang, I'm never certain how many prisoners are in this gang, each landing holds around 80 prisoners, the wing is ultimately run by one prisoner and his generals, called TJ, a big west Indian man about 6ft 2ins and built like a barn door, much of what he says goes.

My cell is on the second landing and not the place to be, because everyone wants to know why you need protection from the screw's, I don't think it will take long before the word is out that I am an ex police officer, but first I need to let people know I am ex armed forces and not to be messed with. There are always opportunities to fight, it is my mission to not have to fight at all, already I know that things can be arranged for a price, like people being let out of their cell when no one else is out, or your cell door being left open for someone to conveniently come and give you an instruction or warning, and by this I mean other prisoners not screws. Most of the discipline or punishment on the wing either by screws or prisoners is carried out in the shower block, and this is where it can get very bad, so when you are allowed a shower it might not always be wise to take one.

There are two things that are now conflicting in me personally, the beast has not yet gone, but for the moment has been put to sleep, and I am now a man of God. How can one man, a new prisoner, gain enough respect by prison officer and prisoners, to spread the word of Jesus, in a place that is clearly the devils domain, and stay in one peace. It is going to take a mountain of prayer and an army of angels, but now this is my commission by God to spread the good news of Jesus Christ, I am now a commissioned and anointed disciple of Jesus. Amen.

There are a thousand questions in my head, how can I serve God with so much hate in my heart, with a beast that would thrive in this environment and, I know I am not as young as I was, but even at 44 years old I can still look after myself, and I am still quite fast. I can hear you saying now, "Freddie I thought you just said you are a man of God?"

Yes that is true, that is to be my path, but it is going to be a long path, very long, and I have so much learn about the God I serve, I only have me, my Bible that Rev Tim gave me and the ultimate teacher Jesus Christ, Tim told me to speak to God all the time and to learn how to know his voice, I have never heard God's voice. There is the chaplaincy in the prison that consists of a priest and his helpers, basically without being ungrateful they are just a first aid team, I cannot get any quality time with them, and only see them in chapel on Sunday mornings, and I have lots of questions that need answers. I will never forgive Max and JJ and one day I hope to catch up to them? I must deal with the beast? How do I make sense of the ordeal that got me arrested? How can a trained marksman shoot an MP5 at me at close range and miss? And many, many more questions that need answers.

Things on the wing are not too bad, I have settled a little, but am always on my guard, many people are very inquisitive to know who I am and what I am in prison for. It's apparently the norm, so I tell them I am in prison for shooting a police officer, and I am a disciple of Jesus Christ of Nazareth. This leaves them very confused and convinced I should be in the hospital, but in general they leave me alone, I have had my first meeting with my legal team and it doesn't look good. I have got charges against me for unlawful imprisonment, having an illegal firearm with intent, possession of an illegal firearm, ammunition with intent to endanger life, threats to kill three separate police officer, and attempted murder, so I don't think I will be going home any time soon. My barrister thinks I could be looking at twenty-five years, that would make me an old man when I get out, there are over one hundred and twenty prosecution statements, and I have to read them all before our next hearing in crown court, I know how serious this all is but I am not that worried, or I am in total denial of the situation or a bit of both.

I have also been visited by a detective inspector in relation to another serious matter involving four of the police officers who detained me, apparently they gave me a really good kicking, unknown to me they were reported by two other police officer and the doctor who examined me, on the night. I apparently refused hospital treatment, they wanted me to make a statement, but I quite honestly could not remember a thing, the inspector said this matter will be dealt with after my court appearances have finished.

So much going on, I am trying to pray to God every morning and every night and some times during the day, I don't seem to get any response from God. I remember Tim telling me that it will come from my spirit, I have been reading my Bible and cannot really make much sense of it, there are some good stories. I have so much time, I do at times get very frustrated with it all, and then the beast come's right out and says, there is no God you know that, and I can feel myself feeling very angry, and now more and more against Max and JJ. Sometimes I wake in the night with terrible nightmares, sweats and fear, it's very strange, all my life I have never felt fear, but since I have been in prison it comes on me very often at night, it happens to many other people as well because I can hear them crying out, and all of a sudden the night screw will bang on the prisoners cell door and shout for him to be quiet. Then other nights it is very noisy for a different reason, when drugs have got into the prison, there is a lot off that and I am amazed as to how it can happen with such a strict regime, the beast loves the night time and one of my prayers to God is that if He is truly there then why dose he not get rid of the beast?

I am learning about free will, my will against the will of God, the only thing that God won't interfere with is our free will. It is said that God will never take away our free will! So, this could be one of the reasons why things get so messed up, and how can I manage that on a day-by-day basis? The Alpha course was very good in respect of being able to ask any question on any subject, and one night about three quarters through where we were baptized, the Holy Spirit came, it was amazing, that tangible sense of a physical presence of God, I want to have that all the time, but I don't get it. The times I do sense the Spirit there is always an amazing sense of peace, I suppose it is because of where I am, and the fact that the beast loves this place especially at night.

There is no sense of time, there are some days I can't tell if it is day or night, or what day of the week it is and I have no need to count the days or weeks, and I have almost resigned myself to the fact that I will at some stage die in prison. I see men getting very angry and upset mostly about what their families are doing or not doing and if their visitors are coming, or even if they get a visit. I am in a good place with regards to that because I don't have any family, it has been so many years since I spoke to any of them, I don't think of them being in my life, I dismiss them the way they dismissed my Dad. As for so-called friends, out of sight out of mind, the screws sometimes ask me why I don't get any visitors, other than my legal team, or my independent psychiatrist; you don't know him do you?

He has been instructed by the court, I call him Prof, because he is a professor and his name is too difficult to pronounce and I don't really like him, my legal team say he has to do an assessment of my mental stability, and my eligibility to stand trial. My team want me to plead guilty by way of insanity, but I am not insane, I am damaged, and have been that way since I was ten years old. Failed by my community, failed by my family, failed by my school, and failed by my local authority. Failed by the armed forces, and failed by the police force!

"Freddie, you are just feeling sorry for yourself!" I can hear what you are saying, and I know we must take responsibility for our own actions and decisions, and I accept that, but how do I know that as a child ten-year-old? My childhood was stolen from me, my teenage years were stolen from me, I was not equipped to be a man, I had no standards, nothing to use as a measuring stick, just hurt them because they will hurt me!

And now just to confuse things even more, I have got the God I have denied all my life! Who would blame me if I really was crazy? And what is a real life like? What is normal? How can people even judge what normal is? How can I possibly be judged in a normal society? A society that even to the present day allows children to be battered, mocked, abused and raped. I know how to duck and dive, I know how to manipulate, I am an expert, I am not shy of challenging work, I have always earned my money I have never stolen it, I am an expert in how to inflict pain, and how to withstand pain, how to survive war, how to use firearms, weapons and explosives, how to dive under the sea, and I make a great cup of tea!

I am an excellent cook, I can cook you a meal or a banquet, I am highly trained in silver service, I have eaten with royalty and beggars on the street, and everything in between, I have had times of great plenty and many times of nothing! Of having a home and living on the street, so just what is normal? I can wash and iron to the highest of standards, and I have at times stunk and been in rags, so just what is normal? In every one of these conditions and states that has been normal for me, I was never shown respect, so I never gave respect, if I did something for you-you can make dammed sure you would have to do something for me, if you hurt me I would cause you immeasurable pain in return.

I have had a message from my legal team that I am in crown court next week to have the charges formally read, and to give me an opportunity to make my plea to the charges, this should make and interesting day. I don't know if I will make it that far, something is going on, the wing is at a state of unrest, I can sense it, the atmosphere has changed and is almost electric. We will be let out shortly for exercise it will become apparent then, it might just be that we have all been banged up for the past five days, because of some trouble that went on. I don't know what it was; the word is a guy got cut up badly for being what they call in prison a kiddie fiddler, or paedophile. They are a species of beings that are hated in prison along with men who beat up women, and coppers (police officer).

The routine for going on the yard is the screws shout down the wing ten minutes to exercise, then if I want to be let out I would have to stand by the door of the cell to indicate I wanted to go out. The screw would come to the door, open the small flap if I was stood facing the door then it would be unlocked and we would in single file go out to the yard. For some reason one of the screws has taken a dislike to me, he has come to the door looked through the flap seen me ready to go, smiled at me and left the door locked. So now I must play a game to find out why I am getting this treatment and if it is only one officer or if it is more than one. I could make a complaint; he would deny it saying I was lying on my bed.

When you want to speak to the screw (officer) it is best to call him boss, and for the few women screws, Miss. So, in this instant I have kicked the shit out the door for the screw to come back to my door, as he has opened the flap he said, "What do you want?"

"I want to go on the yard so do you mind opening my door?"

He gave me a smile that sent a shiver up my spine as he said, "not today you are too late".

I know this is not a good situation, I could continue making a racket till another screw came, but I know it would do no good, the screws name is Mr Fisher, commonly known as 'Fish', he and me get to know each other very well as the weeks and months go by. Back to the now, Fish is on day shift for the next five days so I know I am in for a good ride. For the next five days the only time I am let out of my cell is for dinner each day at five o'clock, just before Fish goes home, and he is letting me out on my own, this is an indication to the other prisoners on my wing that there is something dodgy about me. On the fifth afternoon he knows the screw taking over from him will not play the game with him and I will get let out as normal, and I would be immediately set upon by the other prisoner, because the first place I will head for is a shower, having been banged up for twenty-three hours a day for five days, you will end up quite smelly. So at the end of day five I have to settle the score with Fish or approximately two hundred prisoners will settle it with me on day six.

As Fish unlocks my cell door at about ten minutes past five on fifth day, Fish gives me a big smile as he says, "I wonder if you will be visiting the hospital wing over the next three days scab?"

Calling me scab in a loud enough voice so the prisoners can hear him is a confirmed indication to the other prisoners, that there is in prison terms something wrong with me.

So I reply to him, "I just wonder Fish, but you are about to get three weeks off and not three days!

And as I was saying it I swung around and gave Fish the biggest right hand uppercut I could find in me, he went off his feet and landed against one of the cell doors, I knew I had about one minute before the alarm went off and the whole prison would be put into lockdown and I would be jumped upon by every single screw within one minute running time to my location. So I had to do a good job on Fish to give him the three weeks off I had promised him, I knew the officers coming to the aid off Fish would be coming with long batons, and shackles. There would be no quarter given to me, so I then grabbed him and threw him over the landing railings, and onto the catch netting, this is steel wire netting in the void of the landing to stop people being thrown off the landing.

I jumped in after him for two reasons, one so that from the cell doors through the flap just about every prisoner could see what I was doing and it would give me a few extra seconds with Fish, as soon as we both landed on the netting it was a mighty noise from every prisoner on the wing banging on their cell doors, and because of the intensity of the noise and the alarm going off, I could hear the noise spreading to other wings within the prison, I jumped on top of Fish who was dazed and started repeatedly punching him in the head with both of my fists as quick as I could. I felt the first few baton blows to my back and shoulders then my lights went out and I was unconscious.

I came round in my favoured cell in the block, in complete darkness and I was hurt really bad, I don't think there was any part of my body that was not in immense pain, I felt my head and there were many lumps upon it, and a large cut with dried blood all over it, then suddenly the light went on the shutter in the door came open and I could hear the screws saying to each other, "He is awake". I curled myself into a tight ball on the floor as they turned the key in the lock of the door, the lights went on I clenched my teeth and closed my eyes, two screws stood in the door with at least four behind them.

"Stand up," one of them instructed me and in great pain because my mouth and face were so swollen I answered,

"If you are going to beat me some more you can join me on the floor".

I was just trying to present to them the smallest target possible, "You are not going to get another beating".

"What then?" I asked.

"The doctor will be down to see you shortly and we have been told to give you a shower and some new clothes".

I replied, "No thanks".

The office said, "It is not a request it is an order, so you can either shower yourself or we will do it for you".

Now this was just to get me cleaned up as much as they could so there was less for the doctor to see, I said again, "No thanks".

With that the screws backed out of the door but left it open, then four screws appeared in the doorway in full riot gear and the front two had full length shields, one screw shouted at the top of his voice, "Stand Up and stand at the back of the cell facing the wall with your hands on your head, do it now".

I struggled to my feet as much as I could to comply with the instruction. As soon as I was standing facing the back wall of the cell, there was a massive cry from the screws as they rushed me with the shield and slammed and pined me with the shields against the wall, then the screw screamed at me, "Are you going to have a shower or do you want me and my friends to do it for you?"

I was in so much pain I could not even fall to the floor because they had me firmly pinned to the wall, I shouted as much as I could, "I will have a shower ok."

With that the screws backed off out of the door as I just fell to the floor, I could not stand so I started to crawl out of the door, as I got out of the cell two screws came either side of me took an arm each and stood me up, I was in so much pain, I could see many screws, six in full riot gear, one with a dog that was now barking at the end of a chain, then four other screws then assisted me to the shower and to get cleaned up.

I didn't say a word to anyone I just complied as quickly as I could. Before long I was put back in the cell with what looked like a field dressing on my head, as they shut the door on my cell the light went out and I was in total darkness, I just curled up in a ball like an injured dog licking its wounds. I was in so much pain and I wondered how long this was going to go on for. I noticed that when I was in darkness, there were no cockroaches, and apart from being in pain my heart was at Peace.

I managed to fall asleep for a while then the light went on and the cell door opened, I sat up on the floor and saw the doctor standing in the doorway, he took one look at me and said to the screws, "I cannot examine this man here you will have to bring him to the hospital wing".

I could see the screws were not happy with that, but they had to comply. Then he said to them, "You had better bring him in a wheelchair I don't want him to walk or be dragged".

They were even less happy with that. It wasn't too long before I was in the hospital wing with a four-man escort, and shackled to the chair, when the doctor examined me it was just the doctor and a male nurse, the doctor asked me several times if there was anything I wanted to tell him about how I got my injuries, I just said I had fallen down the stairs. I had six stiches in the top of my head, a broken nose, and my front teeth were cracked and chipped. I had a broken knuckle to my right hand, three broken ribs, and my whole body was covered in swellings and bruising. The doctor said to the screws he was recommending I be kept in the hospital wing for a few days, as I may have had a concussion, but the screws were never going to let that happen, I was kept in the block on twenty-four hour watch.

I was kept in the block until all my injuries were healed, that took twelve weeks in total, there were no charges brought against me and no enquiry as to what had happened, I was not allowed any visitors not even from the Chaplain. I found out when Fish came and visited me one night in the block, just to let me know how he felt, he had been off work for six weeks and he said I should wish I had died. I told him I was going nowhere and that prison was my life, that this might be his place of work, but it is my home now, and that an Englishman's home is his castle, he didn't like it that I was not frightened of him, but at the end of the day what else could anyone do, although my thoughts and actions where not very Godly, I could sense something within me and from what I could understand of the Bible there were plenty of wars in it.

I was seen by the number one governor in the prison and he said, "I want to put you back into general population, but I need to be convinced that there would be no more outbursts of violence".

He is much younger than me and well educated, and making some attempt of stamping his authority on me, but it was not going to work, if there was going to be harmony as far as it concerned me, then he had to address the frequent violence from his own officer, and the very dangerous games people like Fish would like to play, so I gave it to him straight, "Do you think I have to bow down to your authority, you need to get a grip of your own officers, before you will get any help from me, I am going to be in prison probably for the rest of my life, this might be your place of work, but I can assure you it is my home!"

The governor was shocked, let off some steam and sent me back to the block. The regime thought that the block was a punishment, for me they had not lived the life I had, they didn't realize that they judge the block by what they were used to, and what society would think the block was. For me it was a place where twenty-three hours a day I could pray to God, and learn to speak with him and recognize His voice. A place of privacy and tranquillity that I could go deep with God and talk about all the things in my past, that had caused me pain ever since I was ten years old.

I could scream and cry out as much as I wanted to, it was my home and my sanctuary, I had a maid service that brought my meals to me and put them through the door, I had clean linen once a week, and nothing they could do could have any effect on me, I didn't have a single care in the world, and while I was in the block the screws tried everything they could to break me! They could not see that to me it didn't matter if I was fed or not, if I was clean or not, if I was hot or cold, if I had clothes or I was buck-naked. They could come in my cell and kick me to within an inch of my life, if I died I was going to Jesus, I know what the Bible means totally when Jesus said if someone strike's your face, give them the other cheek to strike again. If someone steals all you have, give them your shirt also, the prison system could do nothing with me now, it can only work if there is something they can take from you, or if they could make you to have fear, there was nothing they could take from me and the only thing they thought I would be fearful of was perhaps death, but they were so misguided and wrong. I Had Jesus Christ of Nazareth, in my very soul, I could now speak with him and He with me, it never came from any fancy education and Bible college, university or school, it came direct from God the Father!

* * *

I don't know how long I spent in the block, I had no way of knowing, my legal team needed to have time with me as my court appearance was getting closer, so one morning I was put in general population I had a very nice cell, I had a window I could nearly see out of, at least I could see the sky and know if it was day or night. I had a TV and a radio, I could make tea and coffee in my cell and I had a washbasin and towels. A screw came to the cell and said I was under a strict unlock and was not allowed to mix with any other inmates, if I behaved this would be how I was treated, if I did anything wrong I would be back down the block. They brought my personal things to me and all my court papers and told me I had legal visits all day the next day, so this was the reason for all the good stuff, and the new cell.

The next day my team made my head spin with all the legal stuff, I made my mind up to plead not guilty to everything, I know I can hear you say, "Freddie how can that be?" well this is the way I look at it. I am not guilty of the way they have formulated the charges, I am guilty of some stuff and the charges are all cross related, and most of all I really don't know in my mind exactly what happened, and at the end of the day, I was the only person that was physically hurt! And I feel in my spirit this is the right thing to do, it is totally against advice, but it is the way it must be.

Back to the immediate reality of where I am now, I haven't seen Fish for some time, I don't think he is on my wing anymore, I ask every week if I can go to church on Sunday, today is the fourth week I have not been let out for church, the screws give me the excuse the church is full, I have had a letter from Rev Tim but half of it is missing, I am still keeping up with my prayers and I know things will get better, perhaps when I have finished at court?

When the wing is out in the afternoon for association I am kept in my cell, the screws say it is for my own safety, because the whole prison knows I was a police office, I often get lots of threatening notes put under my cell door, what is going to happen, I am not worried about this at all, and I find it quite amusing in some ways, not that I need to mix with any of them at all. I do have a calling from God to show them the way to Jesus. God has a great mission for me I just know it!

I must be very careful when I get my meals, I am always the last on the wing to be unlocked to go to the servery on my own, as I walk along the wing just about every inmate starts to bang their cell door it can sound like thunder, they chant the same words over and over, "get the pig, cut the pig."

If I was not so close to God I could be worried by it all, but I don't worry what is the worst they could do, give me a nasty death, or another beating, It would be no measure to the death Jesus suffered for me and you, on the cross, don't worry if you are not a Christian or of some other faith, or none, this is not going to turn into a Bible bashing book. This is a story of life and death, I know there is a God because He Himself called me! The biggest problem I have for now is what will I find in my food, so far, I have found, globules of snot, glass, razorblades, small shards of wood or plastic, and the smell of urine, I have a little box in my cell and I am collecting them, I have repeatedly tried to see the governor, but I have been refused every time, so I have got a plan, as the saying goes, there is more than one way to skin a cat. I am just biding my time!

I am positive most of the screws don't like this type of treatment and don't want to be a part of it, one of the female screws in particular, she is very young and I wonder why she is even in the prison service, her main job, or the time I see her the most is when I go down each week to get my change of bedding and clothes. I am not allowed to speak on my little journey and as I get to the counter, to one side is a big linen bin, I have to count my dirty linen into the bin as the exchange is one for one, and the routine is the screw will put clean ones on the counter as I put the dirty ones in the bin, but for me even this is different, but in a surprisingly nice way. As I put my dirty linen in the bin and count it out, nothing appears on the table, the lady screw gives me a big smile, reaches under the counter and passes me a prepared bundle of clothes and bedding, always nicely secured with a clean towel, at first when I opened my bundle back in my cell I thought I would get some nasty surprise but I got a good surprise, in the middle is always a parcel of good food, like fresh fruit, tined meat and sometimes chocolate, and as the weeks go by she always asks if there is anything I need or if I was ok.

So you have to understand there are a few bad and evil people even within the prison officers, but I can assure you most of them are good, and they just have to find a way past, the work of the devil, the lady screw who helps me is almost anonymous because I cannot find out her name, I sense she is a Christian women, when she gives me my bundle, as I walk away from the table I say, "God bless you miss," and she always answers me, "God bless you too Freddie."

So, there is even in this great evil, always some good trying to work its way through!

Another day having been told I have a legal visit this afternoon, I can spring my surprise, as I make ready for my visit I am hiding my little box of tricks to give to my barrister, so she can bring pressure on the governor from the outside. Just as I was about to be taken down, four screws came into my cell marched me outside and my cell was striped and searched, one of the officers asked me what my bundle of papers was for?

I replied, "they are my court papers, I have a meeting with my legal team now".

"Not till we have finished with you," he growled. They opened my papers and found my little box of tricks.

"What is this?" the officer asked.

"I don't know you must have put that there," I replied.

"That's it for you, your visit will be cancelled, and you will be put on a report."

With that they hustled me back into my cell, and everything was upside down, they also took my TV and radio. I could have got really angry and I could feel the beast welling up inside my head, I physically put my hands over my mouth to gag the beast and as the cell door slammed shut, I let out a loud scream. I didn't have the heart to start cleaning up so I just sat on my bed, and in my mind I pictured Jesus on the cross, all blood stained broken and dying, and I could hear His words, with His last breath, "It is finished!" and immediately a great peace came over me and the beast in my head was gone. I lay on my bed in God's presence, without a care in the world, and I must have fallen asleep, when my cell door opened and one of the screws said dinnertime.

I looked at the officer and said, "I am not hungry thanks," and with that he shut the cell door.

I put all my legal papers together, but the rest of it I just left on the floor. I did wonder what would have happened about my legal visit? Just then another screw came to my door and said, "Freddie do you want dinner, they will be clearing they servery in five minutes?"

"I am ok thank you."

I was awake most of the night and the screws were worried about something because, they kept on checking me several times through the night and not just their routine check, I was very drawn to pray, and I felt very calm, almost as if I didn't have a care in the world, and I don't. The night was over very quick and my cell door was opened for breakfast, I didn't say a word to the screw as I got to my feet and slammed the cell door with me still on the inside, I had decided to make a stand about the way I was being treated, if I refused to eat then eventually they would have to take me to see one of the governors.

The screw looked through the flap in the door and said, "I take it from that you don't want breakfast?"

I just ignored him, then about ten minutes later the door opened again and there were three screws at the door.

One said, "What's your problem this morning?"

I refused to answer him, so he tried again, "your cell is in a bit of a mess, don't you think you should clean it up?"

I again ignored him, and they closed the cell door. This went on all day every mealtime, and then for the next three days, on the morning of the fourth day the cell door opened and there were many screws at the door. The lead screw said, "Freddie you are being moved to the block, you can either walk down or you can be carried down?"

I gave the screw a very stern look and just started to walk out of the cell, I knew the way and six screws walked with me, two in front and four in the back, when this happens any personal things are left in the cell and if you are allowed anything then the screws will bring it later.

As we got to the block, I was escorted to the showers, for a second I thought I was going to get a beating, and all of a sudden totally unexpected the beast appeared, I went into a defensive posture and shouted, "you had better go and get the rest of your gang because I am taking at least two of you with me,"

I was totally alert and full of adrenalin the beast had decided that if I was in for a beating then they were going to get hurt. One of the screws tried his best to calm me down, saying, "We just wanted to let you have a shower, before you go in the cell, then we will give you some breakfast and after breakfast, one of the prison governors is coming down to see you".

I was having none of it the beast had me totally pumped up, "bring the governor here and I will give him an appointment with the hospital, and any of you that wanted to go with him".

I had a towel in my hand and I wrapped each end around my knuckles, with that the officers backed out of the shower room and I heard the alarm go off, the alarm means the prison goes into lockdown and at least four officers get into their protective clothing and get out the long shields.

I knew this was all for me, so the beast had me well prepared. After several minutes, the officers reappeared with the riot officers and one of the prison governors, the governor said, "Freddie what is all this about, let me take you to your cell and we can all calm down, and I can stand down these officers".

The problem was that they could not know, Freddie was no longer in control, the beast was and he was all fired up. The governor gave me one more warning but it was a waste of time, the beast was going to have at least one of the screws, before they took Freddie out, the governor backed off and all the shouting started, "Go to the back wall and stand facing the wall do it now".

"Come and get me," the beast screamed out.

"You will not be told again, go to the back wall and stand facing the wall," with that the beast charged the officers, we managed to somehow force our way over the top of the two shields, so we are no longer confined to the small space of the shower room, now we are all in the open space of the block, the screws re-grouped and just off to my right I could see a cell door open and the cell was empty. The beast bolted and as we ran into the cell we managed to slam the cell door shut, me and the beast on the inside and the screws on the outside, one of the screws got his key turned for them to come in on the charge, and I heard the governor shout leave the door locked and stand down. I was relieved but the beast was so angry, as the adrenalin started to subside the beast calmed down and I gradually started to get back control, as this happened I started to physically shake and then I was violently sick, I managed to get the shaking under control and fell asleep.

I don't know how long I was asleep and I don't know what time it is, it is so dark, I could hear someone outside the cell door. The flap opened and I could see it was one of the chaplains, "Freddie would you like something to eat?"

There was a great sense of peace as I replied, "no thanks but could you get me a Bible".

"Yes certainly, but let me get you some food and a cup of tea".

"No thank you just a Bible."

The flap went up and sometime later one of the screws passed me a Bible, the moment I took hold of it I felt secure, a very strange feeling and I knew instantly the beast had been put back to sleep. Over the next few days different people tried to get me to eat, one was even a lady governor, she was very nice. Everything now revolves around if they can get me to eat, if I eat I can have a shower, if I eat I can get my personal things, if I eat I can? If I eat I can? I was getting very tired, the governors were getting very worried because I was not yet sentenced and any day now they would have to get me ready for court, they desperately needed to get me to have a visit with my legal team, but I was having none of it. I don't know how long I have been in this state and there is quite a fuss going on.

The lady governor re-appeared and said I was being transferred to the hospital wing, it was not a problem for me as I had no energy to fight, I got to the hospital wing and had a shower, they gave me clean clothes and I had a nice bed and clean linen. I was still in a single cell it made me feel nearly human again, but they could not get me to eat. I then announced I was going to stop taking water, or any fluids, this definitely put them in a bit of a panic, because I had at this point not been convicted of anything, so the prison was in some trouble especially if I died, there was lots of coxing and nice talk, but it had no effect. I was in a time of limbo and I didn't really know why, I was trying to stay close to God, but I could not even do that for some reason, God seemed far away and I didn't know why, my first court day came and went, I was classed as not fit for court, it didn't really matter because the system is that whatever time I spend on remand comes off my sentence and I knew I would be in prison for a long time.

I was reading my Bible one morning and I asked God, "why have you left me?" and the whole cell lit up with a bright light, I could not see the source of the light, and a very soft voice said, "I have never left you my son, I have always been here," then the light faded, I was stunned how could I miss the presence of God?

This is the work of the devil to separate us from God first in our minds, if the devil can get our mind focused on everything except God and make me chose that, then God will not take way our free will even if we are being duped by the devil, you should understand this is just as it happens for me and I am not a schooled theologian. Once I had worked out in my head that the devil worked in my mind to keep the beast in control of my decision-making then God would have trouble keeping me alive. I had to focus on God and rebuke the devil and the beast; the devil told me I could not rebuke the beast, because the beast is part of me, but I began to realize that this was another trick from the devil, because the beast had been impregnated into me when I was abused and raped as a boy, and God was telling me even in my weakened state that I had the power to cast out the beast, and be rid of him forever. I struggled all this time with how I could do it, I was very weak and getting weaker, everything going on around me was so much of a blur, I could hear the doctor talking to a Governor that they could not legally force feed me as I was not a convicted prisoner, and just then behind the doctor and Governor I could see the light, it was making them look like a they were not really there, I reached out to the light that I now realized was an angel, and thought in my mind maybe this is it, I am going, the Doctor saw my outreached hand and said, "What can I get you?"

I said just out of impulse, "A bacon buttie and a cup of tea." The Doctor looked quite shocked and instantly gave me some water, it tasted good, so for now I have somehow got back control from the beast and have managed to clear my mind, so I can start to eat and drink and get strong again.

Some time passed and I came out of the hospital and back onto general population, but with a difference, the screws have been warned about any ill-treatment, they had nearly lost me and they knew they had to treat me properly. I was feeling good now I have had several interviews with my legal team and we are ready for court, well I am. The team think I should plead guilty and let the court deal with me, but I just don't think that is right, for example I am being charged that in the case of Benny I illegally kept him a prisoner in his own home, that just is not true, I was trying hard to get Benny to leave the flat he just would not go, so how on earth is that unlawful imprisonment?

And so on! My day for pleading came and I said not guilty to all the charges, beforehand the prosecution tried to do a deal with me that would have meant no life sentence and possibly fifteen years in prison, I declined the offer and the crown court trial has been set in eight months' time and planned to last three weeks with all the witnesses being called. So it was just a waiting game and try and survive in general population of the prison. I have got my strength back and I have not had any problem with the beast, God is showing me a specific way of praying and every moment in my cell I am reading my Bible and praying, it puts me in a very special place mentally.

I have put in requests to work on the servery and to be let out for exercise in the mornings and association in the afternoons, the screws are not keen on it as everyone knows I am an ex-police officer, I have been insisting as much as I can, and I feel as if I am making ground, my argument is that I can still look after myself and I have God on my side. They don't like either stand but I think they will let me out soon.

The day has come, I am being let out for exercise this morning but the screws will be keeping a close eye on me. At first there was some sneering as the inmates start to realize I am out with the rest, a few prisoners come over to test the water, one guy comes straight to the point.

"Is it right you are an ex copper?" he asks in a loud voice.

"Yes I was a copper for ten years, but before that I was in the armed forces and in three war zones, and I was brought up on the streets of Liverpool, do you want my autograph or a black eye and broken neck?" I replied so he was in no doubt I was not going to stand for any intimidation.

He gave me a smile and said, "When we do you I won't be on my own".

So I immediately grabbed him by the scruff of the neck and said, "but you are on your own now and that was not a good move was it?"

One of the screws shouted at me from the other side of the yard and said, "Freddie what is going on?"

"Just getting acquainted with some of the local wan-a-bees sir," and put the guy down, that was the end of that and not so bad I thought to myself.

The next few days I was let out on the yard without incident, as I walked around and around I could see that some of the inmates would probably want to get to know me, but would be worried about the consequences of being friendly with me. I still hadn't been given a job, and had not been allowed out in the afternoon, but I was feeling good with how things were going, I was getting lots of time with God and getting stronger and stronger. So the time in prison is slowly passing me by, and from time to time there are issues on the wing, the general alarm goes off about every other day, if we get three days without the alarm it is a good week. I have been getting my meals now at the same time as everyone else, this is good because the rest of the inmates get to see me, and me to see them, this is more important for me as I can assess were any danger might come from, and give the screws confidence that I can look after myself. The dynamics on the wing is always changing, because of people coming and going to court, some don't come back and others do, the ones that do are in an emotional state and I often feel if I could only bring them to know God then I could help.

There are a body of inmates that are called 'listeners', and they are trained by a group of Samaritans that come into the prison every week. Every wing usually has two listeners and they have special badges so that everyone can recognize who they are, and it helps the listeners get credits with the screws, as they are regarded as trusties. I would like to do this myself as for the most part they are regarded by most people to be good and get a lot more freedom within the prison system, the listeners can be called at any time day or night, I have requested through the system to become a listener but the screws have said that could only happen after I was convicted, I don't believe them so I will have to use a different tactic.

I have called to see one of the listeners, I have made an excuse that I am very depressed, the listener is brought to my cell and let in with me for a while, he introduces himself.

"Hi, my name is Richard, I am one of the listeners on this wing, how can I help you?"

I waited for the screw to close the door then I said, "Hi Richard my name is Freddie, I have got you here under false pretences, really I hope you don't mind".

"Not a problem, we can talk about anything".

"My request to become a Listener was turned down, so I thought I should talk with one off you guys".

"That's good because we are always looking for new inmates to join us," Richard went on to say, "we are run by the Samaritans and they come in the prison every week, they do all our training, and we are totally independent of the screws, they don't like that it is a national organization and they have no control over us, once we are qualified we get a lot of freedom to do what we do, but we have to be dedicated and not abuse the system".

Richard gave me some leaflets and told me when the Samaritans came in that week he would give them my name as being interested in joining the group, we chattered on about all sorts of things for hours, and at 12.30am Richard said he should get back to his cell because he also looked after the team on the servery, and he had to start work at 5am. Richard and me got on really well, and I had made my first friend in prison, not that it was my intention, that's just the way it works. So when I was let out on the yard, Richard always came over to me; he also introduced me to some of the guys on the server. The problem of me being an ex-copper soon ceased to be an issue and I no longer had to check my food, and once everyone found out I was the one that did Fish I became a bit of a hero.

Things started to settle down, and during our time of association, I had started a Bible study group, it was frowned upon at first and some of the inmates were not sure, eventually it caught on and we had a good group. We went to the chapel together on Sunday mornings and started hanging out together more and more, the screws even began to like it because there was now less problems on the wing, all the guys on the wing nicknamed me 'the priest', because when anyone had problems I would pray with them and as God told me to I would lay hands on them, and God would heal them or very often give them peace with regard to their own personal circumstances.

So, this became the start of my very own ministry for God, God anointed me and used me more and more, the screws got confidence in me and mostly at night now and again would come to my cell and ask me to pray for them and with them, it was the start of something very special, even the bad guys or the ones who would be bullies had no power against God, and me and I openly asked God very often in a very loud voice to intervene in situations. Whether it be prison inmates or officers it didn't matter, it was God's work and no one could stop it, the beast had gone and I was so free in Jesus Christ our Lord, there was a confidence about me and a hunger to help people. I was invited onto the group of listeners and this gave me more access to people within the prison. When I did my training the Samaritan stand was that if we were of faith – any faith – then we could not use that when speaking to people, unless that person specifically asked for prayer, once my training was finished I have to admit that rule of thumb went out of the window because I started every time with Jesus and finished with Jesus, and I was called all over the prison not just on my wing because people knew that. Time was now flying by and my trial date was rapidly approaching, and my legal team said that the work I was doing would help when it came to my sentencing, we all knew I would be found guilty of something but what that would be was anyone's guess. I was happy in the knowledge that I was going to stay in prison for some considerable time, carrying an illegal firearm on its own is a starting sentence of five years, if the prosecutor had done their job properly it would have given the opportunity to plead guilty, but a lot of the stuff was nonsense.

If you had asked me if I thought anyone could get comfortable in prison? I would have said no and for me it is not just an acceptance of the inevitable, it is far more than that and it is far more than just survival.

My trial will start on Monday morning at the crown court in London, they will take me from the prison at seven in the morning, the only thing that will be uncomfortable for me is being booked out of prison every morning and then booked back in every evening. So I am going to pray all weekend that the Lord makes my way easy and that there are no tricks from the screws. It's an opportunity for them to mess with your head especially on the return trip back from court. I have a great peace in my soul and am not worried, I know God will have everything in hand and my path will be straight.

* * *

The first day in court, so far it is all legal banter between my barrister and the prosecution team, and the swearing in of the jury, it is quite boring but a very necessary process, I guess you have seen the process on TV, the drive in the cattle van coming to court was not too bad, I call the van that brings me back and forth between the prison and the court (a cattle van) because that is exactly what it feels like, my barrister got me a nice new suit, shirt and tie, because I have no way of getting my own things, and I don't know what will happen to them.

The next few days are much the same, and eventually it comes to the prosecution to make its case, I have no direct memory of the event except what is written in the one hundred and three whiteness statement, and that is not a cop out its fact.

I know the full story because I have read it over and over, the prosecution are making the story so bad, and I suppose that is their job. This goes on until the end of the first week and into the second week, at this stage the prosecution ask if I would accept five police statements as evidence, as there are thirty-three in total and they all say much the same. Against my legal advice I agree, and obviously the ones that are left out are the officers that describe me getting a good kicking as I was arrested, I wasn't bothered by that as it is a big enough mess without going into counter claims. My barrister is furious with me and it won't be the last time he gets like that, as I sit day after day listening intently to the story, I form the opinion in my mind that if I was the judge I would lock me up and throw away the key. So I can hear you saying, "Freddie why did you plead not guilty." Well I have said it before, they have been over exaggerating the facts and I am not guilty of all the charges, and the prosecution would not deal before court.

It's day seven in the court and the police forensic scientist is called, he comes equipped with really impressive computer generated visual mapping of the part of the event when the police officer, at the bottom of the stairs fired his gun directly at me, he states there was fifteen feet two inches between the officer and me that we were both facing each other, in a narrow stairwell. The officer was firing his weapon an MP5 semi-automatic weapon in an upwards direction, as I was standing on the first landing, the settings on the officers weapon was set in the second position where on pulling the trigger it would deliver between three to five bullets. He confirmed with his commuter imaging that one bullet went through my stomach, one through my chest and one through my head; the other two bullets went over my head. The scientist went on to say that all five bullets were recovered in the wall and ceiling behind me, it made everyone's jaws drop including the judge. The scientist went on to say further that at that moment I had returned fire with my gun, and shot one round at the police officer, that there were no injuries to the officer and that the bullet could not be found, and that there were no injuries to either me or the officer. WOW!

The judge asked one question of the scientist, "Sir if your evidence is to be believed why is neither the officer or the defendant dead or at least had some sort of injury?"

The scientist replied, "My Lord, I can only produce for you the facts as I found them to be, the only person who could answer your question would be God."

"Do you have an opinion?" the judge asked

"I can only say that on my evidence both men should be dead!"

I think for this to happen to anyone it would have to get you thinking? Well it did me, first I was thinking about the other officer, who had just come to work that night, did he have family, was he married, did he have children, is he still able to work, or did he think it was just another day at the office.

Then I was thinking about myself and what the scientist said in reply to the judge.

"The only person who could answer your question would be God."

Then my own questions "Did God miraculously save both of us?" If He did why? What should I do with all this information? How should I make it change me? How should I present myself now? I know I am going to be in prison for a very long time if not the rest of my life, so why give me this revelation now if only to spend my time in prison?

What good can it do there? The rest of the next few days I could not focus on anything, I didn't hear what went on in the court, or recognize myself travelling backwards and forwards from the prison to the court and back again. On the Friday evening as I returned from the court to the prison I was whisked through the system very quickly and didn't know why, I had to see one of the prison doctors.

"Why," I asked.

The doctor asked me lots of questions that made no sense to me and at the end of it I was put in the hospital wing in a suicide watch cell. I tried to tell them there was no need for it but the decision had been made and that was that. I was put on a fifteen-minute watch, that means someone is sat outside your cell and records what you are doing every fifteen minutes, day and night. By the time Monday morning came I was even more like a zombie, when I got to court my barrister asked me what was wrong, and I told him, he was very upset with the way I had been treated, he had given me a lot of work to go through over the weekend in preparation and I had done none of it.

As soon as the court started my barrister asked for a private audience with the judge and prosecution, so everyone was sent out of the court except for me, my barrister the prosecution and the judge. My barrister was asking for an adjournment for me to be seen by an independent doctor, and he stated I was not fit to continue and asked for a two-day recess. The Judge ordered an instant report from the prison and for two independent doctors, one being a psychiatrist to attend the court right away and then adjourned the court until after lunch, I was put in a quiet cell downstairs in the court building, and I was just dropping off to sleep when I was taken to see the doctors, then before I knew what was going on I was back in court and it was now one thirty in the afternoon.

The court had the reports the judge had asked for, I never got to see the reports myself, then the judge spoke to me direct and said, "how do you feel? Do you think you could carry on?"

I answered the judge and said, "thank you my Lord for your concern, I am tired, but I would rather get on with the case, there have been enough delays."

The judge thanked me and called the jury to be brought in. after the next day the prosecution had finished, and my barrister was not happy. The judge had sent the doctors reports to the prison and I was taken off suicide watch, but kept in the hospital wing, I was still in a daze and not really taking everything in, the next morning I was taken to the court early and as I arrived I was taken directly to a secure interview room where my barrister and his aides were already there waiting for me and they had brought breakfast, bacon butties and coffee, he said we had a lot to get through and began to go through the prosecution witnesses he would contest and as witnesses we would use for me and said basically it would be down to my own evidence.

We went into court about ten fifteen am and my defence was underway, I really didn't see the point because with all the prosecution witnesses no one had lied, they told the story from their point of view. So, what could we say that would be different, my witnesses were more character witnesses, my old

Royal Marine and Navy commanders, My reports from the Police Force and all the training and commendations in my work carrier. So, my evidence only lasted two days with me taking the stand at the end. I was in the witness stand all day and I was totally attacked by the prosecution, my barrister had asked me not to take the stand for that very reason, and at the end of it, it wasn't looking good.

We got to the stage when the jury went out and in the judge's guidance to the jury he brought up one of the charges, aggravated assault and said to the jury they were not to proceed with this charge as the prosecution had not proven this offence by way of no evidence. I was taken to a holding room and my barrister said that if all the charges come back guilty I could expect twenty-five years to life. It didn't seem to affect me hearing that, and I really felt as if there were angels all around me, and my heart was in a good place. My barrister also said that the judge would probably adjourn sentencing for three to four weeks. At the end of the day the jury had not come to a decision on any of the charges and the court was adjourned to the next day.

That night I had a good sleep, and was bright as a button, which seemed strange, the court was continued, and the jury sent out again. About two pm we were told the jury had made their decision and were called back to the courtroom.

CHAPTER ELEVEN

The Verdict

1. Unlawful Imprisonment GUILTY! This was one charge I didn't know how I could be found guilty, the man was a friend, he was in his own home, the reason he didn't come out right away was he was worried as to what would happen to me. If anyone imprisoned him it would be the police because they made it almost impossible for him to come out of his home, by the formidable stance they made!

2. Having an illegal firearm GUILTY! This is a correct decision.

3. Threatening behaviour GUILTY! This is correct decision.

4. Conduct likely to cause a breach of the peace GUILTY! This is correct decision.

5. Having in my possession illegal ammunition NOT GUILTY! The jury found that as I only had one bullet in my gun and at the time I came out to confront the police the rest of the ammunition was in my coat pocket that was still in the flat.

6. Having an illegal firearm with intent to endanger life. NOT GUILTY! The jury decided that I was trying to entice the police to shoot me dead, known as suicide by cop.

7. Three separate accounts of threats to kill. NOT GUILTY this decision is totally bazar?

8. Then the big one, attempted murder on the police officer that had shot at me. NOT GUILY! The jury decided that because the officer fired his weapon first I just retaliated in self-defence, and that if I was out to kill anyone I would have had my gun fully loaded not just with one bullet.

At the end, the jury was discharged and thanked, then the judge shocked everyone by announcing that he was going to have a thirty-minute recess and go straight into sentencing. My barrister tried to contest the judge's decision but was put down, the judge stated there were no reasons to delay sentencing as over the course of time I had been seen by five doctors in total, there were already many statements of evidence on my previous good character. So, no need in his judgement to delay sentencing.

The court was adjourned. I was taken to a secure interview room with my legal team. I must say we were all in a state of shock, my barrister said for Count 1. Unlawful Imprisonment, I could expect five to ten years. Count 2. Illegal firearm, a minimum of five years. Count 3. Threatening behaviour, because of the nature of the whole incident I could expect three years. Count 4. Conduct likely to cause a breach of the peace, two years.

He went on to say that they judge is one of the toughest. So, his total calculation was between fifteen and twenty years. It seemed a nervous wait for my team, but I was totally at peace and felt the presence and the love of God all around me. I could not say anything I just got on my knees to pray, I was thanking the Lord for all his greatness, for the judge and all the legal people involved, for all the administrators in the court and everyone involved, and for all the juror's, I asked God to bless them and their families. Then suddenly that bright light came and filled the room, this time I knew exactly who it was, the soft voice said to me, "You are a son of the living God through the death and resurrection of His son Jesus

Christ of Nazareth! He is well pleased with you; all your sins are forgiven, and you are a new creation in Christ Jesus! You will go forth from this place and be a mighty disciple in all that you do in His name. Amen."

I felt like I was floating, the light faded and my barrister put his hand on my shoulder and said, "the court is ready for us now, the judge will be coming back."

"Did you see that bright light?" I asked, but no one else had seen it. Have I just been dreaming I thought to myself, but I still had the presence of God with me, so I know it was not a dream. We all sat down in the courtroom and the judge came in, his arrival was announced by the court usher.

Then everyone sat down except for me, the judge said that this had been a very strange case, and that he had formed the opinion that I was trying to commit suicide by cop, he was convinced that the help I would get from prison would be good for me and he hoped I would take full use of my time in prison."

He then came to the sentencing, "on count one, TWO YEARS! On count two, TWO YEARS! On count three, TWO YEARS! And on count four, TWO YEARS! All to run consecutive."

Then I was ordered to be taken down, my barrister came to see me briefly in the cell block, and he said, "I really don't know what has happened today, I have never seen anything like it in all my years of practice."

I told him not to be shocked it was the gracious hand of God, we past a few pleasantries for a few minutes and then I was on my way back to prison, but now I was excited because I knew I had a special anointing direct from God, it was amazing.

As I arrived at the prison I was taken straight to the doctor. I thought to myself 'not again,' apparently when someone is given a long sentenced as I have, my mental attitude has to be assessed; I was put in the hospital wing on suicide watch despite my protest to say I was totally ok. After two days being watched I was put back into general population, I can sense a difference in the attitude of the whole prison as I am taken to a different wing, one for convicted prisoners. As a prisoner on remand there is a question mark over your destiny, the jury hasn't said guilty yet! Now I must serve eight years in prison, so with parole I should be out in four years, less the time on remand eighteen months so effectively or potentially have two and a half years, but that time means the system has me, no questions asked.

As I am placed on the convicted wing of the prison, two things are immediately apparent to me! It's, very different, the cons know I am an ex-copper! And the screws are running a very tight ship! (metaphorically speaking) the time is just after breakfast and just before lunch, as I am placed in my cell the screw asked me, "do you want to be let out for association after lunch?"

"Yes please sir" I replied, "Ok on your head."

I knew instinctively what he is intimating at, and after a short while my door is opened for lunch, my cell is on the top level and I have to line up with the other one hundred and fifty prisoners, walk in single file to the serving pantry and then collect my food. The first thing I notice is the only people talking are the screws, "come along and stay in line," then another screw a little further along, "right to the end," as he points his arm in the direction of travel, "down the stairs and no talking," we are led to the end of the wing, directed down the stairs through the pantry for our food and drink on the ground floor and back up to our cell's via the stairs at the other end of the wing.

As I get to the pantry entrance there is a slight level of conversation, as the prisoners in front of me are deciding and asking for their choices of meal, and the replies and chatter from the inmates who are serving. To be a server they must become a trustee, this means that they have been awarded this status by the screws to do menial jobs, and trusted by the other inmates as being ok! As I make my way along the line in the servery, I notice a screw and an inmate at the far end of the servery standing together, the inmate has a name badge and a listener's badge on his shirt, I make my selection and as I reach the end I am stopped by the screw, "stand to the side" as he directs me and at the same time the listener stands with me. I didn't feel any threat the beast has gone and the Holy Spirit is with me.

"I am Cody I am the inmate in charge of this wing and all the workers," and he put his hand out to shake mine, except my hands are now full of my lunch tray and drinks, he smiled at me and said, "That was a bit daft, hey,"

He then went on to say, "You can trust your food to be ok, we don't mess with it on this wing, you are the ex-cop, aren't you?"

I didn't answer.

"It's ok, I believe you are also ex-armed forces".

"Yes," I replied.

"It's ok I am ex-armed forces also, when the wing is let out for association after lunch I will come and speak with you".

"Ok," I said and then the screw put me back in the line, and I walked back to my cell, lunch was ok and I started sorting my personal things out, just then my cell door was opened, it was Cody being let in by one of the screws,

"Is it ok if I come in," Cody asked.

"Yes please do," I replied, and the screw shut the door. Cody started putting me right about the wing, who to watch out for and who was ok, the day to day running of the wing and who thinks they are the boss, and who really is the boss, and we are not talking about the screws here. We had a good chat for about an hour, then the screw opened the door for association, boy the level of noise went right up, as one hundred and fifty inmates were unlocked, this is also the time we are allowed to, take a shower. I didn't rush, Cody had told me to take a shower early in the morning before breakfast, as that is when all the trustees get let out for a shower. Cody said he could get one of the screws to let me out with them, and true to his word that was what he did, things seemed ok at the moment, then the next afternoon when we were let out for association,

I made my way to the ground floor as two pool tables are put out, and thought I would try my hand, as I got to the ground floor I was met by the inmates committee, someone Cody had warned me about, a big Jamaican called Blake – not his real name so I am led to believe – I just think he has probably seen too much TV. I am immediately on my alert as the little group of friends Blake has with him are not of good intent.

"What ye doing down here pig meat?" one of Blake's cronies asked.

I took a few seconds to scan my options and as I looked up behind the locked wing doors I could see at least six screws on high alert, obviously expecting something to kick off. So, I didn't answer, but no way was I going back upstairs.

He said again, "what are ye doing hear white pig trash?"

Then another one of them said, "Ye belong up their man, ye get hurt down here man!"

So, this is the standoff, you would think that now is the time to call the beast, but no I didn't, I called on God. Yes, I know what you are thinking, those of you right now that know Jesus as your saviour, are jumping for joy! Those that know God but of another faith, are thinking this could be interesting! And those of you that are of no faith are thinking not another Bible basher! But just all of you hold on, no matter which camp you are in, first think of this? How many of you have had a police marksman fire an MP5 semi-automatic rifle at you from close range in a closed space and not even got a scratch?

If you can just pause and think for one moment! I know you want to get back on with the story. If you were shot at by a marksman and you did not die, what would you think, it is easy to say, "shit he missed" you can get away with that once, but not five times?????

Pause,

In court it was called an act of God!

So, Blake and his three merry men are ready, willing and able to do me some real severe damage, an army of screws are looking on ready to press the alarm and call a lockdown! And perhaps get to me before I am dead! **Well step forward the man of God!** I took two steps forward and stood as tall as I could, to make a stand to Blake and his men.

"If you will allow me one minute to state my case before you judge me!"

Blake gave the official nod. "It is true I was for some years a police officer, and for many years before that I was in the armed forces, so while you were all learning how to be gangsters, I was learning how to kill people with my bare hands."

I knew that if I don't keep their attention all hell is going to break loose, "I have been reformed by a miracle of God, and I am now a disciple of Jesus Christ of Nazareth."

I instantly thought what if they are all Muslims? Ouch! (no offence intended). "So why don't we shoot a little pool, the screws up there don't have to hit the alarm and at the end of it all if we are not friends we can all go in the shower room and sort it out!"

One of Blake's boys said, "why we now just drag ye little white ass in the shower now!"

Me, "are you worried I might win on the pool table."

Then Blake gave them an instruction that was to save the day, "You all keep ye hands of this little white boy till I have whooped his ass on the pool table."

Some breathing space, I noticed the screws kept a close eye on what was going on. For the next two hours God done his work on them we played pool and I made sure they all won, I told them just about my whole life story, well as much as they needed to know and at the end of it Blake and I became friends!

Well not close friends but good enough, the time came for everyone to go back to their cell, as I was walking up to the top landing a few white boys who all live on my landing came up to me and said, "How did you get to play pool all afternoon with Blake and his boys."

I laughed and said, "Didn't you know Blake and I are cousins, we go way back".

"I have never seen anything like that and I have been on this wing over a year, and have never spoke to any of them, I just keep away."

One of the other guys said, it seemed the event was all over the prison in no time at all. The best part is that from then on no one called me by my name I was called simply. The man of God! And my ministry in the prison was borne.

Being a man of God in some of the toughest prisons in the UK is quite a balancing act between doing what God wants me to do, keeping the confidence with the inmates, especially the ones I would go on and help, and the confidence of the screws who would now begin over time to regard me as trustworthy.

I was quickly recruited by the Samaritans as a listener, I had to do their six-week training course and was firmly told that when I was with inmates I could not talk about God unless the inmate instigated it, then I would be free to talk about God. So I had to fine tune my introduction to inmates I had never met before, e.g. "Hi my name is Freddie I am one of the listeners, I believe you would like to talk with me."

"Yes," he would reply.

These meeting were always conducted in the inmates cell and it could be any time of the night or day and I would then be locked in with that person by the screw, once the door was shut I would then finish my introduction, "What is your name and how can I help you?" Then the inmate would say their name and most of the time they would just need someone to talk to, or they might be depressed.

I would then go on to say, "I am a man of God and a disciple of Jesus Christ," and then ask if I could say a small prayer, and every time the answer was yes. I would simply ask God to be with us as we talked and it was every time good for the inmate and me, even if the inmate was a Muslim, I would use the same introduction, and every single Muslim were great guy's, and we always had amazing conversations.

You see my job as a disciple of Jesus is not to be a Bible basher, or try to convert people to Christianity, it is my job to live my life the way Jesus would have done if he was in my place, and to genuinely love everyone the way that the Father loves me. If people see Jesus through that, then it is up to Jesus to do any conversion not me. Anyone that comes to Christ Jesus, it is their relationship with Him not mine, from that moment on it is only my job to walk with them in case they need my help and so I can be a true brother to them, before God.

You can now imaging I am beginning to get known in the whole prison, the Rota for the team of listeners was quite good and it meant that we would be on call at night about one in six nights As listeners, if we were called in the night and for whatever reason we did not want to go then we could refuse, and as I got to know the screws I let them know that if they got a refusal from one of the team they could always call on me. So some weeks I could be called out two or three times, I found it very rewarding helping people in the night usually with their fears and ghosts, and it was such a privilege to see God at work with them, some even came to make a commitment to get to know Jesus but not all and that was not a problem because it is not my job to convert people its Jesus Job.

There were many miracles that I witnessed whist I was in Westwood Prison and the other prisons I went on to move to, and I want you to have your own opinion to what I share with you. I have been in Westwood for about six months now since I was convicted, and one of the areas the prison officers have encouraged me into is the reception as prisoners come in or come back from court as many are in shock and some can show signs of dark depression and suicide. I have been very good at helping the men and as a consequence it can greatly help the prison officers, I will refer to them from now on as officers not screws, as it is more respectful, at the end of the day they are human beings doing a very stressful and dangerous job. There are a small number that don't do the prison service any favours but they are very few. I will say that the prison officers stand firm together even when one of them might be doing something wrong, and with the team of prison governors it is very much a them and us structure, my stand with the inmates was this, I would not help them or encourage them to do anything wrong against the rules or other prisoners, and I would not grass them up if it was not going to do officers or inmates harm, but if they cross the line with me I would make them regret what they were doing. For example one day one of the inmates on my wing had gotten into a really bad situation with one of the officers and had made himself a homemade knife and at his first opportunity he was going to stab the officer, there was no doubt the officer had treated the inmate badly and without justification, he was one of those officers I was just talking about, but he didn't deserve to be stabbed or killed, so what could I do with this information?

I could go to the officers and warn them, then the inmate would get it even worse, and it would come out that I grassed the man up and I would lose all my trust with the whole prison population and put myself in real danger. I could go to the man and ask him not to do what he was planning and ask him to give me the knife. I didn't think that would work so how was I going to make this stop, that evening in my cell I cried out to God to help me stop this situation. It was about four am and one of the officers came to my door and said, "Freddie I know you was called out last night, and you are not on duty, but there is a guy who seems really disturbed, and we think you would be the best to try and help him, we are very worried he is going to try and hurt himself."

I agreed and they took me direct to the man I had just been praying for, I knew that the man was going to stab the officer that morning at breakfast, so I took the decision to ask for a special request from the officer, "can you pass on to the day shift when you handover not to unlock us both for breakfast, as I know what this man's problem is and it will take me a long time to get through to him."

"Not a problem," the officer replied. As I went into the cell before he could refuse to see me I had slammed the cell door shut, we both knew each other and the first thing he said to me was, "Don't give me any of that God stuff." I told him I was not going to do that but that I knew he had some problems and I would like him to share them, we was in his cell all day we never came out for breakfast or lunch and we nearly got to blows with each other several times, by mid-afternoon we were both getting hungry, but I knew we could come out at tea time because the officer was on early shift and would have gone home by two pm. when we got our food we went back to his cell as I was not going to leave the man till it was all sorted out, I eventually got back to my cell at ten pm and had a plan I hoped would work, I asked the night shift officer if in the morning I could speak privately with the officer in question as soon as he came on duty and before breakfast, and good to his word the officer came to my door about half an hour before breakfast. I told him I knew what he had been doing to this inmate and asked him if he could stop riding his back, as it was making him very ill.

"I wondered why you was in there all morning yesterday."

I pleaded with the officer and just said, "He cannot take you riding his back anymore">

The officer tried to justify himself and said he would think about it. Before he went I asked if he would allow me to pray for him, he was hesitant but he agreed. I knew God would do a job on him, the man with the problem didn't get out for breakfast and when I checked on him he was sleeping, about eleven am the officer came back to me and said, "I think you might be right Freddie I may have been a bit tough on him I am going to speak with him."

My heart went in my mouth as I did not yet have the knife, "Just a minute can I have a few moments with him first just to smooth the ground".

"Ok".

I gave a sigh, and he let me into the man's cell, as he shut the door right away he gave me the knife and asked me to get rid of it, he said, "I have only got three years left to do and if I got more time I think I would lose my whole family,"

I was jumping with joy and praising the lord, I then told him I had spoken to the officer and he is going to come and have a word with you if that is ok, the officer went into see him and they spoke for about ten minutes, I stood outside just in case, I could not hear what was being said but as the officer left the cell I saw them both shaking hands, I was so delighted and thanked God for making everything work out ok.

Some weeks have gone by since that episode and the wing I am on has become very routine and in many respects quiet, Blake who had become friendly over the past months has now been moved. As inmates we never find out why people go, we get up one morning and they have already gone, except when people may have finished their time and go home. I was in a meeting for all the listeners just after breakfast, it is our monthly meeting with the Samaritans were we talk about what has been going on, and any information the Samaritans might have for us, then in the afternoon we have role play and training, it can be quite fun and I always look forward to the time we have with our Samarian volunteers, today we are informed that our listener leader will be going home in two weeks' time so Cody will be leaving us and we have to vote in a new leader in the prison.

The Samaritans decide that we should have another meeting the day before Cody leaves and then we can take the vote, we all get two ballot cards and have to put the names of the listener we would like to take Cody's place, so it can be voted in at the next meeting, I have got to like Cody over the time we have worked together in the prison, and I know he will go on to do good things when he is out. The two weeks pass very quickly and when we go in our normal meeting room, we get a shock, the Samaritans have transformed the room and there is lots of party food and even some of the governors and prison officers are there. We have had a good day and when it comes down to the vote it is me that has been voted in as senior listener in the prison, the number one governor is with us and he seems quite happy with the decision. It is quite a good move for me and it will look good on my prison documents, but as you will find out I become quite demanding of the prison governors, and I look at it this way we save the prison staff a lot of work, especially at night and I think we should be rewarded for it, we should have some perks.

Well Cody got a good send off and he was missed for all of about one day, that's not being nasty that's just prison life, we don't really make friends in prison you just get on with people and have a strange level of respect for each other, so my time as number one begins and I have talked the governors into having progress meetings every Monday morning as that is when the Samaritans do their rounds and it is a way of bringing up the profile off what we do, the next thing I asked for is a listeners room, this is a space on the end of each wing that can have tea and coffee in it and some nice chairs, so that when we are asked to sit with people it is first a better environment, and safer for the listener, and the room I have requested is a room right by the officers station room, there are windows so the officers could see in but, they are locked so that the inmates are secure, and one of the problems we have experienced is that on occasions when we have been in a cell with inmates, if there is an incident and the prison goes into lockdown then we can be in that cell for many more hours than we need to be. The next thing I ask for is security passes for listeners, this would take the form of a small pass that we pin to our shirt just below our listener badges that allows us movement around the normal wings of the prison without an escort, making it easier for us and freeing up the officers for other duties, the current method of movement is that if I am needed at another part of the prison then an officer has to come and get me, then escort me through all the gates to where I am needed, but there are prison officers at all the gates so if we had passes giving us authority to move freely then once again if frees up the escort officers.

I have to put all these suggestions to the Samaritans first and get them on board, because it is them that have to get the requests cleared through the prison governors. The Samaritans are not keen on the ideas because they have never done anything like that before, and the balance between the Samaritans and the prison officers is a delicate one, so at the first hurdle my proposals fail, but I have been praying and I get very bold and at one of our governors meetings I just by accident let the proposals slip, and would you believe the number one governor goes for it. After some time it works very well for everyone, and even the prison sceptics come around to it in the end, it leads to greater confidence for us as listeners and a greater confidence from the prison officers to us, and it gives us a big responsibility to make sure it works.

* * *

I would like to think that all these good ideas were all mine, but I have to say that they come to me after a time of prayer, and as prisoners we get lots of time in our cell to pray for hours, I know you will probably think that all prisoners have TVs, DVDs and radios, this is not the case, so we get even more time when the prison is on a lockdown, because on a lockdown there is no movement around the prison. Lockdowns are called for many reasons, mostly if they think they have lost a prisoner or one might have escaped, then during the lockdown every single prisoner is counted, this usually comes about from a clerical error on behalf of one or more of the prison officers, if it is because of a disturbance or fore a form of discipline then it will usually last for three or four days. I can take advantage of this to pray and read my Bible. When I was fifteen years old and getting kicked out of school, if you would have told me I would enjoy lots of time to pray and read I would have laughed at you, but here I am doing just that every day.

So, the next challenge for me is to secure a new cell. On the first landing near to the officer's station is a cell that is quite a bit bigger than the normal cell and it doesn't get used for multi occupancy, so I will have to use some spiritual influence to get it, I need the bigger cell because I have collected quite a few books. The tactic I am going to adopt is that it will be easier when I am called out at night.

The one thing I have noticed about prison life is the amount of people who are in prison because of mental illness, this environment cannot be good for these people, and won't help their behaviour change when they get out. I have met a guy, I think he is about fifty years old and very uneducated, he is in prison for criminal damage and shoplifting, he has been in prison for the past thirty years and he loves it because everything is done for him. I believe that when he comes up for release the officers must physically put him out of the gate, because he is so scared about being on the streets. He has no family or friends on the outside, and as soon as he is put out he is homeless. So, the format is that when he is out on the street he will steal from the shops knowing he will get caught, in fact making it so much easier for them to catch him, then if the police say no action will be taken he will smash a window or two.

The consequence is that he is put back in prison, then when he is back in prison, he will refuse probation, eventually he is given six to twelve months, then the cycle will repeat itself, all over again, very sad really that this man is so institutionalized. It is my belief that he has been in prison most of his life, for minor theft or damage, it's so sad. When I have spoken to him about how this all started, he simply says, "When I was twenty I got depression." As a society in the twenty-first century we need to be doing much more.

I have sown the idea of my cell move to the senior officer and I have said a pray, so I know now it will happen. I know that most of you probably think I am crazy and you might be right. I don't think it is all a coincident that when I pray, what I pray for comes to pass. I have recently had calls more and more to the medical centre, or the hospital wing as it is known, there are some really sick people there, and I know I can do some good. The chief doctor is a good man and I have started to build some trust between us both, one day I put our new movement passes to the test, as in small print at the bottom it says, (access to all areas except D wing and the medical centre), and as I spend a lot of time at the hospital wing I pushed the boat out and chanced my hand, I walked up to the gate at the entrance to the hospital and just raised my pass and said to the officer, "Good morning boss I hope you have a good shift, I have just come down to see some of the inmates".

"Ok Freddie," He replied as he unlocked the gate.

As I entered the hospital one of the staff said, "Thank goodness you are hear Freddie we were just going to send for you, one of the guys is diagnosed with hallucinational behaviour, as he is suffering the result of many years of serious drug abuse."

I have spoken to this guy before and he responds well to me, so I am shown to a strip cell where he is being kept, he is creating a storm and the officer on duty wants me just to talk to him from the door. So I just told him, "if you chain someone up like an animal, then don't be surprised if they act like one, I will be ok to go in to him, and in any case you have got him trusted up like a chicken ready for the oven."

He then lets me into the cell, the man is going crazy, I simply put my arms around him and told him everything will be ok. Instantly the man calmed down, the two officers standing in the door said, "How do you do that?"

"It's not me, but God." I replied.

The guy then sat on his mattress totally calm, so I asked the officers if we could take off the jacket of his restraints just to make him a little more comfortable, there was a pause but then the officers unlocked the padlock holding the jacket in place. I thanked the officers and then they left and closed the cell door, thank you Freddie the guy cried out, "I have been like this for three days,"

I asked him "what did you do?"

He answered, "I am not sure I was just talking to myself and they didn't like it."

"I think there must have been a little more to it than that," I said.

But the guy insisted that was it. I stayed with him most of the day and had my lunch with him and when I left him he was fine, I went back down to see him a couple of days later and I had been praying for him a lot during that time. To my surprise, he was on a ward and in normal prison clothes, one of the orderlies came to me and said, "I don't know what magic you used on him, he is so different, and he is taking his medication without a fight".

I just repeated myself in answer, "It is not me it is God".

On my wing, I have a small group of Christian guys that I have identified individually that they are Christians, but they won't say that to anyone else, so I have got them together to chat and hopefully pray together. When I asked them why they will not be proud of their stand with God and go to the chapel on Sunday morning?

I was shocked by their reply, one of them said, "You really don't know why so many inmates go to chapel on a Sunday morning, and why on some Sundays it's really packed out?"

"I assumed it was just the way that God was working in the prison," I replied.

They laughed and said almost collectively, "it's not God working it's the drugs working, Sunday morning is the only time inmates from other wings have contact."

"Yes so why is that so relevant?"

They went on to explain, "It's when all the deals go on, drugs, messages, and the like,"

I am not only shocked I am upset, "

So if you took all the drugs away and all the messages, how many inmates would really be in chapel?"

"Probably just the seven of us," they replied and laughed again

"So the Chaplain thinks he is doing an excellent job?"

"Yes, he is, he is helping people get messages and drugs all around the prison."

In my state of being shocked we got on with our little meeting and we formed our prayer group, at times it was difficult to meet, and the officers were a little suspicious of us at first, so we managed with the help of the Chaplain to be allowed to go to the chapel on a Wednesday evening after dinner. It was very good for many reasons, and I think this was also only possible because of the trust and the work I was doing in the prison.

I needed to address this issue on a Sunday morning and I have been praying about it, the chapel can hold about two hundred inmates when full, as it is most weeks. The escorting officers, once every one was in the chapel, left with just two officers sat down by the doors, so I understand now how this can happen. I was beginning to know how Jesus must have felt when He went into the temple and cast out all of them that bought and sold in the temple; he turned over their tables, and said to them, "It is written 'my house shall be called the house of prayer'; but you have made it a den of thieves." (Mathew 21:12) So what can I do? Should I go into the chapel and expose all the dealing going on, somehow, I don't think that would work, for either the inmates or the officers. But I do feel offended by this information, so after a lot of time in prayer God has given me this quest. For the next week from Monday as I work my way around the prison doing my normal work I will spread the rumour with all the main characters on each wing that on Sunday once everyone is in the chapel there is going to be a raid by the officers, before the service starts, looking for drugs. The word definitely got about, on the next Sunday there was only twenty-two inmates in the chapel. I had also on Sunday morning suggested to the duty officer for the chapel that he should search everyone on the way out, all twenty-two of us where searched so the word would go around the prison that the search did happen, and so instead of looking bad and causing a riot I had got more confidence from the inmates and the officers, and more to the point kept the Temple of the Lord clean.

But I could not do that every week, searching twenty-two men doesn't take long but to search two hundred would cause a problem, so the problem hasn't gone away it has only been interrupted.

As a disciple of Jesus, I can no more stand by and let this problem persist, no more than Jesus could have his Father's temple defiled 2000 years ago. I do pray a lot more about this and get Gods guidance, and I am aware that my little prayer group are watching me also, there must be some questions being asked by the Chaplain and the officers as to why suddenly the church congregation went from two hundred just to twenty-two?

I know I won't get away with the same trick again, and if I seek out anyone it will be noticed, It's Tuesday now and its constantly on my mind about what will happen on Sunday. I have had a message via one of the officers that the Chaplain would like me to see him. That's not good; if I get caught speaking to the Chaplain it might raise some eyebrows. I make my way to the Hospital wing to speak with a few inmates, when I get there as I go past the strip cell I can hear someone in a bad way on the inside, immediately as I walk pasted the door my spirit is dampened in a big way. I feel sick to my stomach and very unwell, as I get to the office I make enquiries about the man in the strip cell, the officer tells me, "He has been transferred early this morning from another prison to be assessed and we are waiting for the doctor to come and give him liquid cosh." Liquid-cosh is a nickname for a concoction of drugs that will knock a man out for three days, it is only used in extreme circumstances, and after the three days the man will be in a calm state for about four days while the drugs wear off.

The officer goes on to tell me he is a spit an' and biter, and defecates his cell at every opportunity, I asked if he was convicted or on remand, his reply was he is on remand for criminal damage and resisting arrest but has yet not entered a plea at court. He is only a young man of thirty-three years of age, I felt so sad in my spirit, a feeling I had never felt before, and my feelings were so intense. I am going to call this guy Legion.

I could not focus on what I had come to the hospital for, so I decided to go and find the Chaplain, I met the Chaplain in the centre of the prison where all the main wings meet, I was still disturbed about Legion and knew I had to try and help this man, but how? The Chaplain asked if I had got his message and I said, "I am just on my way to see you."

He asked if I would go with him to his office and I complied, as we went past the control station in the centre of the prison I let the duty officer know I was going to the Chaplain's office if they needed me. On the way there I kept on asking myself all those questions about Legion, and the officer gave me the information freely, they never do that. It was as if he wanted to, and I noticed that as I got close to the door Legion stressed out even more. When we got to the Chaplain's office he said to me, "Freddie are you ok you seem very distant?"

I replied, "No. I'm very concerned in my spirit," and then told him about Legion, he didn't seem bothered about it and just went on to talk about Sunday.

I just said, "Not many people there this week".

He kept pushing me for answers but I acted as if I knew nothing, he intimated at one point that I was trying to sabotage his service and he was not going to allow that to happen. I got quite annoyed with him and was just about to let the beast loose on him, but I suppressed the beast and bit my tongue.

I asked the Chaplain to pray with me for Legion, but he had anger towards me in his heart and sees my now as a threat, so he declined to pray with me. I knew that whatever evil was in Legion's cell was very bad; it had started affecting me and the Chaplain. I went back to my cell for lunch and as soon as I was on the wing the bad boys wanted to know what I was doing with the Chaplain. I just said he was asking me why so few men went to Sunday service, I asked him to pray with me but he refused. I got my lunch and went to my cell normally, the officers will leave my cell door open but I wanted it closed, after I had eaten I got on my knees and cried out to God, I read from my Bible, Mark 5:1-20 where Jesus cast out the demons from the possessed man. I knew then what I had to do, and I knew only the living God Jesus could do this for me. To the surprise of the officers I chose to stay in my cell all the rest of the day and night and I prayed and worshiped God and asked him to fill me with his holy spirit. The officers were concerned because they had never seen me like this before; I just assured them that everything was fine that I just needed some self time.

The next morning after breakfast I went straight down to the hospital wing to check on Legion. As I went into the hospital wing my spirit was immediately in a state of high alert. I went to the office and the duty officer said, "Freddie we had just put out a call for you". They explained to me that lots of the inmates in the ward are complaining of a great fear and overpowering feeling coming over them. Two medical staff had gone home feeling ill.

I asked how I could help, and they asked me if I could just be on the ward and comfort the men in there. I said I would and I also asked for some more listeners to be brought down, and the officers complied with that request. The other listeners came to the hospital, two of them and right away and said, "What is going on?"

They also could sense something not right, the three of us set about talking to the inmates on the ward, and it seemed after a while to calm the men. I went back to the hospital office and asked about Legion, as I passed his cell door he was screaming and crying out, but in a language nobody could recognize. What I could sense was the beast in me being aroused, I rebuked the beast and sent him away. The officers in the hospital were at ease telling me what was happening with Legion, they said that yesterday the doctor came in the afternoon and gave Legion the biggest dose of liquid cosh he could. But it had no effect, the officers were surprised but

I wasn't, I knew I had to do something but no way would the officers allow me in the cell with Legion.

I asked if I could walk outside his cell and pray, and the officers said yes but I must not lift the flap on his door, or make any attempt to talk with him, as I started to pray outside the cell Legion became more abusive and louder, it was distressing to hear the young man in this state, but I just kept on praying, and reading scripture from my Bible. I walked back and forwards outside his cell all into the evening, but it had no effect on Legion at all. The next morning I went back to the hospital wing and again started walking back and forwards outside Legion's cell, once again he became worse with me outside, one of the officers made the comment, "I don't know who is the most crazy him in the cell or you on the outside."

And he asked me how long I would keep praying outside Legions cell, I answered him, "As long as it takes".

The next day was the same and still the liquid cosh had no effect, the doctor was baffled, and the officers said they had never seen anything like it. I just kept on praying and reading my Bible, on day five of this episode, the officers revealed that in six days he had to be ready for court and that they didn't think it would happen as there had been no change in his condition. I asked if I could just speak with him from the flap in the cell door. I just felt compelled in my spirit, the officers were reluctant, then to my surprise the senior officer said why not, nothing else has worked. He told me that him and another officer had to be with me and we would have to stand behind a shield, so I agreed. We all stood behind a shield and as another officer released the latch, the smell was overpowering; all of a sudden lumps of shit hit the shield and the officer asked how had he got out of those restraints. Legion was shouting out in many different tongues and voices, saying they are the devils angels and that we had no power over them. The officer holding the shield pushed the shield against the door so nothing else could come out, and the senior officer was just about to shut the flap when I shouted, "I am a disciple of the living Christ Jesus, and I have authority over you all, desist and be gone from this man, in the name of Jesus Christ of Nazareth, the risen son of God, and by the power give to me through the Holy Spirit I command you to be gone in Jesus Name."

As I said Amen the cell filled with dark smoke, at the top of the cell is a vent to let air in and as I kept my hand over the flap of the door the smoke went out of the vent. Then the man who was Legion collapsed to the floor.

I turned to the senior officer and said, "it is over, you had better get some medics to this man".

They quickly took the man out and now I renamed him, Phillip. The medical staff took him under guard and got Philip showered and cleaned up, he was very dazed and in a confused state, then they put him in another strip cell but without the restraints. The officers called me into the office and said, "we are going to have a problem writing this up, we have broken just about every prison rule going".

"Then don't report what you have seen, pretend it was a dream and just say Philip came out of it himself, or it was a delayed reaction to the liquid cosh, but whatever you write remember you have just witnessed the power of God first hand."

I never did find out how the officers recorded Philip's miraculous recovery, I know it was all God. Several days later Philip was on the normal ward and the next week he went and attended court. Again I don't know what was said in court, except that the officers from the hospital wing let me know that all his charges were dismissed, and he went home to his family. Praise God.

* * *

The prison governors realized the problem with inmates going to Sunday Chapel and dealing their drugs and a new system of applying to go to Chapel was introduced that made it impossible to use the Chapel to deal. The numbers dropped right down to about only fifty inmates every week, and all the credit for the detection of the problem went to the Chaplain.

As the days and weeks go by, another thing I was able to introduce with the help of the governors, is that a listener is allowed every meal time to stand at the end of the servery, in order that if any inmates need to speak with a listener then we can put them on our daily list to be seen during normal daytime hours. This was to reduce the amount of night time call outs, saving the listeners and the officers time, and that way the night time calls can be kept for real emergencies. Since we adopted this system I am only getting called out on average about once a week.

There has been an incident recently when God called me out in the middle of the night. I was in a deep sleep and I was woken up by a movement in my spirit, it was strong, and I was very disturbed, this has happened to me before and when it happens in this way it has usually meant a death in the prison. I started to pray and asked the Lord who I should be praying for? I knew there were several men in the prison that could become suicidal at any time, and I knew of two people who had been on visits and it had gone badly, or the visitor didn't turn up, this can be a particular problem in prison from time to time. As I was seeking Gods guidance in prayer, the officer on night duty who was the turnkey, came to my cell door and unlocked the door and said, "Freddie who is it you need to go and see?"

I was quite taken aback as he was on his own, and he is not supposed to unlock any cell at night, only in the case of an emergency, and he should have two other night duty officers with him.

I instantly said, "we need to go to the hospital wing". At that point I was just being led by the spirit.

The officer replied, "Come then let's go".

I could sense the hand of God in control, as we got to the hospital wing, I looked at the accommodation board that showed where all the inmates where, and my eye was drawn straight to a single cell and a man we will call, 'Laurence'. I said to the turnkey officer that is who we need to see, as we looked into the cell, Laurence had started to hang himself.

The officer unlocked the cell and between us we managed to get Laurence down, but he was not breathing, I started CPR and the officer got on his radio, raised the alarm and had the control room ring for a paramedic. It seemed as if it was no time at all and the paramedic was there, the turnkey officer and I had got Laurence breathing again, but he was still in a bad way, they took him off to hospital with a police escort. The turnkey officer thanked me for my assistance and asked, "How did you know Laurence was trying to kill himself?"

So I turned the question back on him and said, "How did you know to come to my cell in the first place."

I knew it was God's work and the assistance of His holy angels, but I left the turnkey officer to ponder about it himself and as I was taken back to my cell I was worshiping God's greatness, and wondered how the night officers would record this incident?

About two weeks later the same officer came to see me and he had the Chaplain with him, I was invited to go with them and we went to one of the common rooms had coffee and sat down for a chat. The officer was relating to the Chaplain exactly what had happened the night we saved Laurence's life, and said that in his report he could not involve me as it would have led to difficult questions. He went on to say he had been waiting for about eighteen months for an important promotion, and that he had just been informed that his promotion was coming through and also a commendation for his work in saving the life of Laurence. Instead of feeling joy he was feeling guilty, because he put everything down to me, we talked for some time and I was surprised by the change in attitude from the Chaplain, this is all the workings of God and I told both the Chaplain and the officer that fact.

Just before we finished I said to the officer, "Do you know Jesus?"

He answered, "No".

I went on to say, "Would you like to get to know Him as your saviour and your best friend?" and he said, "Yes".

I then lead the officer in the presence of the Chaplain and of God, to our Lord Jesus, I gave him some things to think and pray about and then went back to my cell as happy as happy could be. The Chaplain told the officer, who was near to tears and full of the Holy Spirit, that he would take me back to my cell, at first I thought this was for my telling off, but I dismissed the thought and said to myself, no one will take my joy. As the Chaplain and I got to my cell door the Chaplain stepped in the door and in astonishment to me he said, "Freddie I have never seen anything like that, and you are truly an anointed man of God, and I would like it very much, if you would let me speak with the number one governor, and arrange it for you to work with me in the Chaplaincy."

"I would like that very much." I replied.

I was having such a high I could hardly contain myself, and felt we were taking much important ground from the devil, and I need to let you know this is only a small insight into my life whilst in prison. Despite all our gains, it is still for the most part the devil's domain, sadly!

And then to add to my euphoria I received a letter. Whilst I have been in prison other than legal visits I have only had one, I have sent visiting orders out to people, but they never came, so I quickly understood why prisoners would despair, but this was a letter from a mother of one of the young men through my ministry with Jesus I was able to help. You remember Philip, his mother sent the letter and it was short but to the point, it simply said.

Dear Freddie,

I am the mother of the young man you helped in the prison hospital, my son's name is Philip, I felt compelled to write to you to say, I don't know what you did with him, but thank you for giving me my son back, he is reading his Bible every day and coming to church with me every Sunday, May God bless you.

A very grateful Mother.

I was so happy to get the letter and that evening when I was in my cell worshiping the Lord, my cell was full of the Spirit of God.

Things in the prison have been going very well, the governors and the officers are pleased with the work of my team of listeners, and the new system of being available at the servery at meal times is really helping, the Samaritans are also very pleased with the work we are doing.

Then one evening at dinner all hell broke loose, any prisoners that are under a special watch – which can be for all manner of reasons – are kept back to come to the servery one by one, at this particular time there are four inmates on this list, so they are let down one by one. The very last one was a very young man, I don't think he could be more than eighteen or nineteen, very small almost like a boy. I knew he had been getting quite a hard time off some of the officers, like how I started. Being refused showers, exercise, and visits. He has been on the wing for about four or five weeks, and I had tried to contact him, but the officers were keeping him out of bounds to everyone.

I had managed to find out he was on remand, waiting to go to court and his name was Peter. As Peter was let out of his cell he was the very last inmate to be served, during the week at dinner time there is always plenty of food left over because several inmates who are attending court that day are on the list for dinner, if they don't come back from court then there is always plenty of food left over, and although it is not allowed, we always plate some meals up for the night staff. As Peter is making his way from the second landing he is escorted all the way down by two officers, I am standing just outside the servery on the ground floor, and I was disturbed to see the verbal intimidation this young lad was getting. I could not make out what was being said but I could see, by the body language it was not good. Peter entered the servery and I stepped inside the far end where he will exit and be escorted back to his cell. One of the selections on the servery is roast pork, and believe me there is lots of it left; what I want to remind you of is this is the very last inmate to be served.

As Peter came to the roast pork he asked the inmate serving for some pork, the server put a nice piece of pork on his plate, Peter asked if he could have another piece of pork, so the server obliged him and put a second piece of pork on his plate. As soon as the meat hit his plate one of the escorting officers who was stood just in front of me, shouted, "only one piece of meat," and told the server to take off the second piece of meat, I could sense in my spirit this was not going to end well, as the officer was just in front of me I said to him, "sir there is lots left over".

To that he answered me, "Stay out of this, you governors scab."

Now I know it is not going to be good, in my mind I am screaming for Jesus and Gods intervention, Just at that moment Peter reached into the counter and took the very same piece of meat that had been taken from him, the officer in front of me began screaming at the top of his voice for Peter to put the meat back. Peter gave him a look of defiance and started to walk out of the server. The officer exploded in a rage and with his hand underneath Peters tray smashed it in the air and all over the floor, and screamed at him to get back to his cell. Peter said nothing and began to walk up the middle set of stairs, closely followed by the two officers, as I stepped out on to the ground floor landing I saw another two officers going up the stairs at the end of the landing.

I knew what was going to happen, Peter was in for a good kicking, I pleaded with the officer in charge of the servery to hit the alarm in order to stop what was about to happen, he refused and instructed be to get into the servery, I ran past him and hit the alarm button that sends the whole prison into lockdown. I screamed at him that he has to stop this, at that moment I could see the four officers start to set about Peter, on the second landing, I ran up the centre stairs and along the second landing I could see Peter already unconscious but still being kicked by all four officers. I screamed at them to stop, and as I engaged with them I put two of the officers over the railings and they landed on the catch net. I simultaneously pulled off my T-shirt as I could see a bad bleed on Peter's head.

I jumped on top of Peter in an attempt to protect him and applied pressure onto his head wound with my shirt, the remaining two officers continued kicking out and getting me instead of Peter. At that moment the duty governor arrived on the scene and stopped the assault. It was a lady governor and as I kept the pressure on Peter's head wound she looked totally horrified. I screamed at her to get an ambulance and a doctor or this man will die. She radioed the control room for the ambulance and another officer took over the compression on Peter's head. I was then frog marched down to my cell and for my part that was it, some hours later the lady governor came to my cell and thanked me for my help with Peter. She had no news as to his condition other than he was stable in hospital and his family had been informed. She then asked me for my listeners badge and my movement pass and said I was suspended from free movement due to an enquiry. I informed her that I had not yet eaten, and could I be allowed a shower and some clean clothes as I was still covered in blood. She said she would see what she could do, the officer that was with her interrupted and said, "There is no food left, I will bring you some clean clothes, you can wash in your sink." My cell door was then closed.

I was praying long into the night, when my cell door was opened and four officers stood there, I asked, "what is going on?"

The senior officer said, "You are being taken to the block, and in the morning, you will be charged with assaulting two officers".

At that point I knew there was a massive cover-up being performed, and I was going to be made the scapegoat. I went down to the block peaceably I had had enough drama for one night. When I got to the block I informed the officers that I had not eaten and that I need a shower and clean clothes, he didn't answer and just pushed me into the cell, I couldn't help myself and said, "What is with the pushing, shall I change my charges to three officers?"

As I stood up to him I could feel the beast being released, I quickly clenched my Bible, the officer saw that I was resisting and he said, "Give me that book".

So I handed it over and I said to him, "The next time you open that door you had better have your full body armour on".

He slammed the door shut and turned out the light, I was at first outraged, then I could hear the cockroaches coming out, I stamped my feet to make them scurry away, but they would come straight back, then the word 'armour' kept ringing in my head over and over, the lord was making me recall in the Bible, the 'Full Armour of God', Ephesians 6:10-20. I started to recall it and was shouting out the words at the top of my voice.

V10. 'Finally, my brethren, be strong in the Lord and in the power of His might.'

V11. 'Put on the whole armour of God, that you may be able to stand against the wiles of the devil'.

I knew this was the work of the devil, so I said it again.

V11. '*Put on the whole armour of God, that you may be able to stand the wiles of the devil*'. The cockroaches had gone and although the cell was pitch black and I could not even see my hand in front of my face, as I closed my eyes a great peace came over me and, in my mind, there was a bright light, it was just as when I was first visited by God! I opened my eyes and pitch dark, I closed my eyes and an amazing light, I continued shouting out the scripture,

V12. '*For, we do not wrestle against flesh and blood, but against principalities, against powers, against the rulers of the darkness of this age, against spiritual hosts of wickedness in the heavenly places.*'

V13 '*Therefore take up the whole armour of God, that you may be able to withstand in the evil day, and having done all, to stand.*'

V14. '*Stand therefore, having girded your waist with truth, having put on the breastplate of righteousness,*'

V15. '*and having shod your feet with the preparation of the gospel of peace;*'

V16. '*above all, taken the shield of faith with which you will be able to quench all the fiery darts of the wicked one.*'

V17. '*and take the helmet of salvation, and the sword of the Spirit, which is the Word of God;*'

V18. '*praying always with all prayer and supplication in the Spirit, being watchful to this end with all perseverance and supplication for all the saints,*'

V19. '*and for me, that utterance may be given to me, that I may open my mouth boldly to make known the mystery of the gospel,*'

V20. 'for which I am an ambassador in chains; that in it I may speak boldly, as I ought to speak.'

I just kept shouting these words from God over and over until eventually fell asleep, I woke up with the noise of the officers taking around the breakfast, but they never turned on my light and never came with my breakfast, so again I kept repeating out loud the words of God, over and over, I was in a great place with God, then some time later my light went on and the cell door was opened, four officers and a governor that I had never met before, stood there, the governor said, "Listen to me carefully, you are charged that the said time and place you did assault two prison officers without provocation, and that furthermore did threaten another officer with his life".

He went on to say, "these are serious charges and you will be going before a panel of governors later today, do you have anything to say to these charges?"

As I was about to speak the cell door was slammed shut and the light turned out, I just continued to pray to God, I knew that this could go very bad for me, so I just stayed close to God and kept the beast under control. I think about one hour had gone by and my light went on and the cell door was opened, again four officers stood in the doorway, one of them threw to me a towel and some clean clothes and said, "Come on now, you can have a shower and put on your clean cloths, you will shortly be going to see the governors".

I threw the towel and clothes back at him and said in reply, "No I won't I am not going to that kangaroo court and you can shove the shower up your ass," and I slammed the door shut and just continued praying. I had decided to go on hunger strike and to stay dirty, so we would be at a standoff, and there would be nothing they could do, so this went on day after day, I had a sink in my cell and a toilet so I could keep myself alive for a long time, my aim was to get justice but not to die. I was very smelly and the officers kept me in total darkness, but would you know it the cockroaches never came back, it was as if it was a sign from God that He was in this with me. I knew that if they took me to the governor in the state I was in then they would be for the high jump, I wasn't going to get cleaned up just, so the officers wouldn't look in a bad light, this is the state they have kept me in, so this is how everyone will now see me.

The standoff has already lasted several days I think I am gauging that by the number of meals I have been offered, because I have no way of knowing. The light goes on when they want to speak with me or offer me food. It won't be long before the governor makes a personal appearance. The officers had sent for the Chaplain to get him to try and get me to co-operate but I sent him away, two of the Samaritans have tried to see me also, but because they are from an organization outside the prison, the officers would not let them see me in the condition I am in. My spirit is strong and I am in constant prayers to God, or when I am not praying I am sleeping, it has begun to get very difficult to gauge time, and I feel as if I am losing weight. I am still being kept in total darkness, and I have got to a stage where when the light goes on for a few seconds it is painful, the officers will be starting to get concerned, not so much for my welfare but in case they get caught keeping me in the conditions I am in, and they have definitely underestimated my resolve.

I am thinking also about the young man who got beaten, he must have been in a bad way, I keep asking about his welfare, the officers just say they don't know who I am referring to and say the fight was with me and the two officers I put over the railings. I know the whole incident is being twisted around, whatever happens I will not let this go, the officers will feel they can keep this up for a long time because I don't have visitors and very little contact from the outside would, the only people that can kick up a fuss on my behalf are the Samaritans, and I don't know how far they will go, for the most part they stay out of prison politics and prisoners' rights. I think now I have been in this condition for about eight days and nights, and even now the cockroaches have not come back.

Many more days and nights go by before there is any change and eventually the day of reckoning comes. It starts with breakfast, the light is put on and its left on, this is quite painful to my eyes, the officers are really, trying to be nice and to get me to have a shower and a shave and get cleaned up. Something is definitely different, I am very week and they bring a doctor to see me, the doctor is someone I have not met before and must be new to the prison, he deems me to be underweight but well in the circumstances, I know the doctor will have to make a separate remark on the holding documentation, and he will be very careful not to attach himself to the situation in case I die and there is an inquest. They only other thing that he has said is that I have got muscular deterioration. I know this happens when your body has no fat reserve left to turn into energy and it starts to use up muscular tissue to keep vital organs working. So I know I am getting to the point where the officers have to do something and that they will now be getting concerned. I get a visit from the Chaplain and he pleads with me to get cleaned up, but for all his pleading I will not change my stand. I did make one request of him, and that was for him to ask the officers if you could get me my Bible and would they leave the lights on so I can read it. He prayed with me for a while but I just stayed on my bed, as I am too weak to get up. I could see in the Chaplain's eyes he was very stressed by the way I was being treated and I asked him to find out about the condition of the young man that got beaten up, he said there was no official record of it, and I was then violently sick.

As the Chaplain left my cell I could hear him giving the officers a piece of his mind, I had never heard the Chaplain raise his voice before, and he stated that he was going direct to the number one governor. The officers came back to my cell and were almost pleading with me to get a shower and cleaned up. What they didn't realize by now is that I was not physically capable of doing anything now.

A short while later the Chaplain returned with the number one governor, and he hit the roof, he shouted at the officers, "get this man out of there right now and get him down to the hospital wing, I could not move now so the officers had to get a trolley, they put me on it and started me on the way to the hospital wing, the Chaplain stayed with me and the governor said he would come back later to see I was ok, when I was in the Hospital wing a different doctor examined me and told the staff to phone for an ambulance, so I was a little dazed as to what was happening. I remember being handcuffed to a trolley when the paramedics had arrived and put in an ambulance. I laughed at the ambulance man and said, "do you see how stupid these people can be, they chain me to the trolley have two officers guarding me, and think I might have the strength to run off, when I haven't even the strength to sit up,"

I think at that stage I was either given something to make me sleep or I passed out, I don't know, I woke up in a hospital bed in a private room, with two prison officers sat at the end of my bed, reading. Then a nurse came in and said, "Hello Freddie how do you feel today?"

I replied, "I don't know yet, but I feel as if I have had a good sleep," and I saw I was on several drips and asked what they were for.

The nurse explained, "This one is to keep you hydrated and for any drugs we may have to give you, then this one is to give you food supplements if we have to and you keep refusing to eat."

Then she went on to say, "the Doctor will be in shortly to see you, would you like me to arrange for you to have a shave and get rid of that, Robinson Crusoe beard?"

"Yes, please I replied."

I tried to sit up and realized I was shackled to both sides of the bed, I just laughed to myself, one of the officers looked at me struggling to sit up and said, "sorry about that but it's the rules."

That also made me laugh that now all a sudden they want to play by the rules, as I sort of came to recognize why I was here, I began to get very angry, the two officers were right in the firing line and I was trying hard not to let go at them, I had never seen these two officers before and asked where they were from, they wouldn't reveal anything.

I got my shave and all cleaned up, I had several official visitors from the prison service and they came to the bizarre conclusion that I had manipulated the whole of this episode to try and escape prison, well talk about closing ranks, every time I spoke about the guy who got beaten they said I had made it up to fabricate this plan to escape. I was shocked.

On returning to prison I imagined I would go back to the block and the whole process would start again, but it wasn't, I was rushed through reception, my feet hardly touched the ground, I was put on a new wing, I had a nice cell and a TV, the senior officer on the wing gave me his pep talk, "We will treat you with respect and you will treat my officers the same, while you are of good behaviour the TV will remain, you will have your meals brought to you. You will not be allowed out of you cell, except for your shower that you will have to take before breakfast, and in the afternoon for 30 minutes exercise. If you have any questions you will only address them to me, have you got that?"

"Yes, but you are treating me as an 'A' class prisoner and I am only a 'B' class," I answered him.

"No, as of this morning you have been re-categorized to 'A'".

With that he shut the door, I knew this would go badly for me and I would probably not be able to change a single thing. To get to see a governor I would have to put in a written request, I asked if I could have some request forms and to my surprise I have been given them. The next morning, I was let out for my shower and I handed the officer my request to see the number one governor, the officer took the request from me, he was with three other officers.

I joked with them saying, "I only need one off you."

And one off the other officers said, "you are on a four man unlock, so don't be expecting to get out very much."

As I came out of the shower I noticed that my request form was in the bin, so I knew I was not going to see anyone, I was also informed that I could not have any visitors such as the Chaplain, listeners, Samaritans, and even legal. I knew this is against prison policy but if I could not get to a governor then I just had to put up with it. I decided to chill out for a while and sit it out, to see what happened. Two weeks have gone by and I get my shower every morning, and all my meals, but I don't get me exercise in the afternoon. Every day I am told that there are not enough staff, I have been putting in requests to see the governor without any response, so I must sit it out a while longer, but it is getting difficult, the good side of things is that I have my Bible and plenty of time to pray.

Another six weeks have gone by and the routine has stayed the same, and they are starting to get to me, I have asked for my outside visits and phone calls and have been declined, not that I had anyone on the outside to talk to.

Then came the big move! It's 6am Saturday morning, my cell door is thrown open and I am in the middle of my prayers, there are so many officers at the door I can't count them. The senior officer says to me, "you have one minuet to get dressed, you are being moved."

"What do you mean I am being moved, where am I being moved to?"

"You will find out when you get there."

I was about to try and discus my move and the officer took one step back and two officers stepped forward with full riot gear and shield, and behind them the dog and handler, I quickly came to my senses and got dressed, the officers would not let me ask any questions. I was taken direct to the yard by the reception, as I got there I was put into leg restraints and chains and handcuffs, there were six officers two in riot gear, the dog and handler, and two more officers standing by a big black Range Rover 4x4. I was tempted to kick off, as I didn't have any idea what was happening or what they were going to do or were I was being taken. I just asked, "What about my personal thing and my legal papers?"

"That will all follow you."

I knew this wasn't normal especially on a Saturday morning. Then in a flash I was pinned down, I saw a medic coming towards me then felt a needle go into my right arm, right away I became light headed, I was put in the middle of the back seat and the leg shackles where locked to a ring on the floor, two officers got in the back, one each side of me, so I was sandwiched in the middle then two other officers got in the front and the last thing I saw was the prison gates started to open, then my lights went out.

I am awake now and in a new cell, it's quite noisy and I guess its lunchtime, on my bed is clean towel and clean prison clothes, I have got one hell of a headache, and went back to sleep. as I was sliding into sleep I looked up, the cell has a very high ceiling and at the top of the outside wall I could see a barred window and remember looking at the sky thinking that's nice I hope it isn't a dream.

When I next wake up it is very dark and I have no idea what day or time it is, and I go back to sleep, I feel as if I am suffering the mother of all hangovers, on my sink in the corner is some plastic cutlery and a plastic mug, I manage to drink about three cups of water then went back to sleep. I am woken with the cell door being opened there are six officers and a dog outside, the officer says, "Pick up your clean clothes and your towel you are going to have a shower and on the way back you will get your breakfast".

I said in reply, "You don't need all this, I won't do anything to give you cause to use the force you think you need."

As we started walking along the passage to the stairs the dog handler said, "We don't know you from Adam and we can only go by what is on your reports, but I can assure you one false move and I will set the dog on you".

I replied, "There won't be any need for that boss".

As I finished my shower the officer said you put all your dirty clothes in that big blue bin in the corner, when you get back to your cell with your breakfast there will be clean clothes and towel already in your cell.

I thought that was quite good, I asked if they could tell me where I am, then another officer said, "When you are escorted out of your cell you just do what you are told when you are told, and you will be fine, there is no talking, this time we will let it go."

I wanted to ask lots of questions but did not want to get on the wrong side of them, for the moment I have a room with a view. I get my breakfast and was escorted back to my cell, 'no talking'. As the officer was closing the door he said, "You are in Highwater maximum security prison, give us no problems and you will find out it's an ok prison."

I was just about to ask a question and the officer pre-empted me and held his hand up, to indicate for me not to talk, and said, "Enjoy your breakfast."

The officers where very firm in their actions and I would love to see what was on my papers, what stories and lies had been written down, well I guess that's me with no chance of parole was my first thought, I should be up for my first attempt at parole in about twenty-two months, I am supposed to be going down the ladder not up, they have put me up to an 'A' cat, not good, the breakfast is very good though.

The days are very strict routine, I don't get to talk with anyone, on a Monday morning as I go for breakfast there is a table laid out with various request forms and visiting orders, you have to take what you want and write them out and hand them back in at lunch time, any reply you are entitled to is then given to you in writing on the next Thursday morning. If you don't get a reply then you can take it that whatever you requested was refused, sometimes the request will come back to you with a big red stamp across it saying 'DECLINED' and you get the message.

I have been here over six weeks now and I am still on a six man and a dog lockdown, it's frustrating to me, and the officers must get very fed-up of it, because it is a complete overkill. I have requested to put my frustration to the governor and have had a reply to say my request has been granted but it doesn't say when. In this prison it is very strict keep your mouth shut and be patient, two weeks after my request was granted, I not only get to see a governor but I get to see the number one, I am taken to a very nice office and told to sit in the chair, it looks like a posh visiting room, after a few minutes a very big women comes in and as she goes to sit in the chair opposite to me she asks all the officers to leave, and says', "I will call you when I need you."

All the officers leave the room; she has a big file on her lap and says, "Is it ok if I call you Freddie?"

"Yes mam," I reply.

"You don't have to call me mam, I am Jenny Whitehead. You can call me Jenny or governor," she went on to say this is your file here and it is quite impressive and I am confused as to how you suddenly set about assaulting two officers to be brought here. She then says, "You may speak freely".

I went on to tell her the full story, she was very lay back and open, and after I had finished giving her the whole nine yards blow for blow she said, "Freddie I am going to investigate what you have told me and thanked me for my honesty, she also had my listeners badge and movement badge in the file and stated that, that was what was confusing her, an attack on two officers in the way it had been reported was totally out of character, and if it had have been true, why were there no police charges of assault.

Jenny then made some phone calls and had me put under a new regime, I was not taken back to the cell I was in I was taken to a new wing, by just one officer who was openly talking with me, he informed me that the level of security that I was under is the highest and the only person that can change that is the number one governor. I was taken to my new cell and all my personal things were already in my cell, it was quite a strict wing but it is to be expected as I am in a maximum security prison. Over the weeks and months I had many talks with Jenny, mostly about the work of the Samaritans, who worked in the prison, that had asked on many occasions if they could have a team of listeners, one day I was called into a meeting with the number one, and the Samaritans, to talk through the possibility of having listeners and if I would mind being in charge of them, I was so pleased and said "yes" without a second thought.

So it was agreed and it was to be a trial on my wing first, and eventually expanded throughout the prison, the Samaritans were so pleased and said they had been trying for many years to be allowed to have listeners, and now all of a sudden they can. I just said God has a mission for this prison, and I was soon working with the Chaplaincy office, that was great, Jenny also after some time agreed for me only to have a movement pass, it was a great time and I got to know a lot of the officers very well, the tough regime made it easy for me as there were not so many lockdowns, as most of the inmates were on long sentences and for the most part co-operated with the officers.

* * *

I am due for my parole board but I am still an 'A 'cat, Jenny had informed me that she could not change my category due to the information on my documents in relation to the fabrication of the assault on the two officer, and that it was unlikely to change. I was actually fine with that because the work I was doing was in my own prison ministry and once a month in the church the Chaplain would let me deliver the sermon. I had quite a following and when I preached the chapel was always full, I was doing good works for God and the prison and I was happy, I did wonder if I was becoming institutionalized. Whatever it might be it was a good time in my life, and God was also using the time to work with all my ghosts and the beast has never been seen here. God gave me an exercise to write down all the hurt in my life especial as a child, then when I had finished through prayer before God we took the pain and the anger one by one cast them out of my life.

It was an amazing time of healing over about the next year, then the next exercise I did before God, was to write down all my non forgiveness, starting with my family for not letting me see my Dad when he died and for me to say goodbye, It is an amazing freedom and release to be able to forgive, I have to admit I am struggling with the forgiveness of my abuse and rape, this is very difficult. And I know we also need forgiveness so that our Father in heaven can forgive us, through the death and resurrection of Jesus Christ.

I have a great relationship with the inmates in the prison as I did with the increased number of the listeners. We have helped a lot of men, there is a large Muslim community in the prison, and I am equally involved with them from the work of the listeners as with anyone else in the prison, and it is good comparing and talking about our differences in faiths. One man said to me that he liked the fact that I didn't try to convert them to Christianity, so I informed him that was not my intent or job before God. I simply said to him that I am a disciple of Jesus and it is my job to live as good a life in the image of Jesus as I can, and then if through what you see in my life, you would like to get to know Jesus better that would be between you and God and the Spirit of God, but that if that did happen then I could help. None of the Muslims that I spoke to whilst in prison did come to know Jesus as their saviour, but one man did write to me after he had left prison to say I had helped him so much that it had now been possible for him to return to and reunite his whole family, I was so happy to get that news.

I met many people in prison and there were so many miracles whilst I was there, and my time especially at the maximum-security prison is flying by, and the fact that I see so many men working their way through their sentencing, is a wonderful thing to see. There seems to be no way I can get the lies on my documentation changed. I have even tried to get my legal representation to get involved but with no effect as they say that it is a prison system not a legal system. So, it looks like I am stuck with it, on my last parole board I was asked if I still denied the assault on the two officers and the minute I said "yes" my parole was declined. It is so crazy, so I just go on doing God's work in my prison ministry, in the knowledge that eventually when my eight years are finished they will have to let me go.

I only have eighteen months to go, and I have the respect of many people in the prison, officers and inmates, I was allowed to see a document by one of the senior prison officers just the other day that showed some very interesting statistics. I was not supposed to see them but he wanted me to see them, the paper showed figures from the prison review, that in the years before the introduction of the listeners scheme there were on average nine suicidal deaths per year, and in the first year of the scheme there had only been one suicide, and for the three years since there had been none and only one serious attempt. Of cause, this was being attributed to the work of the prison officers and staff, he showed me the document because it was his opinion that it was more down to the work of the Samaritans and listeners. I asked him if he could show that to the Samaritans and he said he already had, but that he just felt it was only right for him to let me know, and that I could not bandy this information about because it would land him in a lot of trouble. I have been very busy in the prison and I especially spend most of my time in the hospital wing, because that is where the most need is. I am still surprised by the number of people that are in prison from situations that have risen from some form of mental illness, and I don't believe that the system that we now have in this country under the umbrella 'Care in the Community' works. Prison for many people is the result of that failure, and that society and the medical profession have to get away from the attitude, of smothering every problem with suppressive drugs, this is not the answer. If we were driven more by a person centred help and dealing with their problem, rather than smothering the problem with drugs and label's, then I am positive there would be more people that get well, and less people that are in our prisons.

If you take me for an example when I was growing up I needed people to recognize there was something seriously going wrong in my life, and that I was not stupid, lazy or thick, and that simply finding a convenient label for people's problems is not fixing a problem, it's compounding the problem. If you label someone and convince them that they own that label, then that is the way that person will behave, and they will become that label. I can say this from a position of confidence, with the amount of people I have helped to get well simply removing the label, Schizophrenia, Bipolar Disorder, Depression, and many more, labels. And working with the person and their doctors to reduce and in some cases completely end their dependence on medication, and then dealing with the root of the problem.

Through the grace of God, the power of the Holy Spirit and my own determination to stay alongside that person till they are through whatever it is they have to face, and get rid of whatever beasts there are in their life, and for them to formulate a healthy response and attitude away from blame and condemnation, to allow themselves to be loved and made well, to see themselves the way that God intended them to be, and to have a positive hope and realization for their future, even if they have to spend many years in prison, they can still have a life, and start to build now, to keep them stable when they are released, then that has to be good.

* * *

Despite all the odds, I have got rid of my beasts, I have faced them and cast them from my life, I have not forgotten anything, but I have, by the grace of God, been able to make the memories inactive in my life. They don't hold any power or pain, the chains that bound me are broken and it has all been replaced with the most immense love from God.

I am now only eighteen months away from my release and I have just come from a meeting with the number one governor and the leader of the Samaritans, the Samaritans have asked the governor if I could attend their three day annual conference, this would mean I would be out of prison and in a hotel, unsupervised, the governor informed us that to be allowed out of prison, I would need to be a 'C' cat status prisoner and I am still an 'A 'cat status, so just as my hopes were built up and then dashed, the governor came up with a plan.

She said, "Listen Freddie I am going to take a massive risk with you, one that if it goes wrong could cost me my job! Because of your dedication to the work you have done constantly over the years in this prison, on the weekend of the conference the Thursday afternoon you will come and see me, I will de-categories you to 'C' cat, on the Friday morning at the reception office you will be given a three day overnight pass, then released from prison into the care of the Samaritans, they will take you to the conference for the three days, with some spending money, and in your own clothes, and you will return to the prison by 10am Monday morning, from the reception you will be brought direct to me and I will make you back as an 'A' cat prisoner."

I was speechless and then the Samaritan leader went through all the do's and don'ts. I was so excited my heart was pounding in my chest, and this was going to happen this weekend, WOW! I could not thank them all enough, the Samaritans then asked if I could give a small talk on the Saturday and the Sunday of the conference about how life is in prison as a listener. I was happy to do anything that would help, and I re-assured the governor that I would not let her down.

The end of the week came very quickly, the other thing I had to do was keep this to myself and not to say a word to anyone, only a certain few officers would know and be involved. Thursday came and the governor recategorized me to 'C' cat, I could not sleep all Thursday night I was up most of the night in my cell, praying that God would protect me, and I would not be tempted at all, and that I would get back on time on Monday morning. Friday morning came and one of the senior officers came to collect me and take me to the reception, I was showered and they had cleaned my civilian clothes, when I was changed I felt good I had my overnight bag and ready to go, my weekend pass was given to me with the conditions I had to adhere to. On my way out of the gate the senior officer slipped me an envelope and said,

"I could not think of a better inmate, more worthy of this than you and don't open that envelope till you are out of the gates,"

He patted me on the back and gave me a big smile, as the gates closed behind me there were, three of my favourite Samaritan friends waiting for me with a car. I didn't know who was the most excited them or me. It was six and a half years since I experienced freedom, no shackles, no one giving me orders or instruction, they allowed me to sit up front in the car, and I felt so good, I looked in the envelope the officer had given me and it had eighty pounds in it, and a short note to say the officers had a whip round for me so I could treat myself, and a card saying well done. I was even feeling a little emotional, one of the Samaritan ladies sitting behind me passed me two envelopes and she said one is from the number one Governor and the other was from the Samaritans, I opened the one from the Governor first it had a nice card that just said, thank you for all your hard work Freddie, and it had a fifty pound note in it, then the card from the Samaritans was much the same with one hundred and fifty pounds in it, and it said it was from all of them.

I was now quite emotional and had to take a few minutes to compose myself. We talked in the car about what was going to happen in the conference and that there were several ex-prisoners who had been listeners that were coming to the conference, but that I was the very first person that had been let out of prison to attend the conference, and they went on to say that outside of the conference I was as free as a bird and I could come and go as I pleased, I was so happy.

We arrived at the conference centre, after driving for about two and a half hours, we all registered and got given our own conference packs and badges, I was shocked as mine was a VIP pass as I was also one of the speakers. I thought this was just going to be a small event, but they were expecting about five thousand people, from all over the country. I got to my hotel about one pm, just in time for lunch, I was booked into the hotel full board and five stars, there was quite a lot of people at the hotel that I started to meet, and I was like a mini celebrity as all the Samaritans from around the country had been told I was coming out of prison. I was also pleased to meet up with some old friends from my previous prison and was able to fill them in with what had happened, as they had been told nothing by the prison staff.

I slept so good that evening and was up early for my prayers, and looking forward to the day, I managed my presentation ok and I was told it went down very well, the next day Sunday the presentation was even better, and for the whole conference it was amazing seeing how much work the Samaritans actually do throughout the country. It was so informative, I also got on well with the people who had been listeners in different prisons around the country, they were amazed I had got out of prison on license for the conference, and some of them were putting on bets whether I would go back. I reassured them I would definitely be going back, because a lot of people had put a lot of trust in me.

Before I knew it the conference was over and Sunday evening in the hotel there was a bit of a social gathering, I was invited by several people to have a pint or two but I informed them that I was out on trust, and I had not had a drink for nearly seven years and if I did have one it would probably spoil my whole weekend and I was happy on soft drinks. The weekend was a great success and after breakfast on Monday morning the Samaritans got me back to the prison on time, as I entered the prison one of the officers that is not so pleasant was shocked to see me coming into the prison under my own steam.

He said, "Where have you been?"

I just gave him a smile and said, "On holiday."

I could see the confusion on his face and then I was quick marched through reception and taken to the number one's office, she was so happy to see me, and I bet she was also relieved. I was in her office for about an hour as she insisted on knowing everything about the weekend in detail, then it was back to my cell. When I got to my cell I was quite exhausted and was just about to have a sleep when one of the duty officers came in my cell and said, "Freddie could I go and see a man that was feeling suicidal".

I smiled and replied, "Yes I'll be right with you", after all this is exactly what the weekend was all about, helping people in their lowest times.

I was also informed by the governor that she had to put my status category back to a (A) it was no problem to me, but I did think it made a bit of a mockery of the entire system. There were many comments over the next few weeks, and everyone I spoke with could not believe I had been out for a whole weekend, especially from an (A)cat prison, that's the power of God I told them.

Some months later I was again called to the Governor's office, she once again had a big smile on her face, whatever next I thought as I walked into her office. I remember it was a Thursday morning about eleven am.

"Have a seat Freddie," she said.

"Yes mam," I replied as I sat down.

She went on to say, "As you have proved yourself to be totally trustworthy I can no longer keep you as an (A) cat prisoner, so we have worked out that on Monday next you will have only one year left of your sentence, so I am re-grading you to (D) cat and on Monday morning you are being transferred to Latchmere House Open Prison, and from there you will be allowed out to work each day, so you can start to put your life back together."

I was stunned and so happy I could have given the governor a big fat kiss? Ok not quite.

That night in my cell I was thinking of all the things I could do, my mind was running away with me, over the next few days I was busy trying to get around the prison to as many people as I could to share my news and say goodbye. I had worked hard in this prison and had many friends who I knew that now I was a new man I would miss them all, including many of the officers. Monday morning could not come quick enough, two of the officers that I got on very well with volunteered to drive me to Latchmere House. It was so relaxed, none of the normal shackles I had got used to, there car was outside the prison and I was allowed to walk out under my own steam, no guards, no shackles and no dogs. I walked out of the gate across the car park where the officers were waiting and then we were off. I was so happy to be going to Latchmere House as it was near to Richmond Park, and I knew that was not far from the church people that had helped me so much at the start of my sentence all those years ago.

* * *

It is quite strange that God the Father (El-Elyon) The Most High God, would bring me back to a place were a lot of my abuse and rape began 41 years ago, you must understand that Max was born here and this is where his parents used to live. I was brought to this park many times in the summer months, under the guise that I was on holiday with Max visiting his parents. What people never knew was that Max's parents were never home, they would always be away, I never ever met them. So, to come right back to this place seeds very strange, God is obviously going to show me some important things through my remaining year.

CHAPTER TWELVE

The Final Year

After my initial assessment in Latchmere House Open Prison, I have asked if for my day release I can go to work at the church that had helped me so much in my first year in prison. The church were happy to accept me on their staff and all the necessary paperwork was submitted, my request was granted and it meant that I could leave the prison Mondays to Fridays from seven am to seven pm, it was so good coming out of prison every weekday morning, on Saturdays I had a free day and I could leave the prison from nine am to six pm and go wherever I wanted to go, provided I was back on time.

Sundays were lockdown for everyone, if anyone wanted to go to church on Sunday morning it had to be the local church to the prison, except for me, I managed to get a special license to attend the church I worked at. The church had three morning services, eight am, nine thirty am and eleven thirty am, then a service in the evening at seven thirty pm, as I stated to the number one governor, I needed to attend all the services, my special Sunday license was from six thirty am to eleven pm, only God could arrange all of that. When I went to see the number one governor to get my licenses, he said, "Nothing like this had ever been granted before in the history of the prison, and that I had better not let him down."

I never came back late ever, and I stuck to the rules to the letter, I didn't want to give anyone any excuse to revoke my licenses.

***

Whilst I was at the open prison and working at the church many things on a supernatural level happened, my special licenses for a start. At the church I started working with people who came to the church who were ex-prisoners, they were always shocked when they found out I was still in prison. I quickly got to know a lot of very good people at the church from all sorts of backgrounds, and on Sundays between the morning services and the evening service, I would always be asked to Sunday dinner by one family or another. On several occasions I was invited to dinner by a High Court Judge and his wife. We always had great conversations about the courts and defendants and prison life. It was like a window of genuine concern across the full range of the judicial system, not that we could change anything I think we were both enlightened in many ways and understood more from both ends of the spectrum.

In the church there were so many beautiful people and families, just trying to do their best for the kingdom of God, and I started to get a new prospective of God's work and His unfailing Love for us all. I could spend a lot of time telling you what went wrong in people's lives and the mistakes that people make and the bad decision making that happened, but if we are all honest with each other we are all guilty of many things, and in the Kingdom of God there is no condemnation. That is why Jesus died on the cross, so that we can through the simple act of saying sorry to each other and we will be forgiven of all our sin. This in itself is a massive subject, and I will touch on it again later, for now let me tell you that God has a sense of humour.

***

It's now 2004–05 and I have been invited to join many church leaders and other people, to pray and talk about how we can collectively help a mission coming to Clapham Common in the summer, the mission is *Just10* an initiative by the then Rev J. John, a great charismatic and funny man of God. The whole theme is to demonstrate the Ten Commandments in a very modern way and show people just how important and relevant God is in today's world, and that it is more important now than ever before that we get that Jesus is the Son of God and he did die and was resurrected so that we may have eternal life with the Father through the gift of the Holy Spirit. So how do I demonstrate Gods humour?

So here I am coming out of prison and going to prayer meetings to pray for the mission and to help with the logistical planning of the event. To put a huge marquee tent in the middle of a common that at that time was riddle with crime, and keep it safe for fourteen days with all the equipment in it, to be able to seat about three thousand people, with a total value of around one and a half million pounds, and very little money to play with.

Because of my military and police background I was asked to oversee the internal security, basically once everything is set up it is our responsibility. Well I can see the picture in your mind right now a great big high fence lots of security guards, especially at night, maybe a couple of guard dogs. Well you can clear that from you mind here is the humour of God, remember I am coming out of prison each day on license, and now I have to ask the governor of the prison for special permission to come out at 6am and return at midnight every day for fourteen days, because I am head of security for a mission worth one and a half million pounds. I can see you gasping right now, and for those of you who have some knowledge of prison systems you are now thinking, not a chance.

You would not be wrong in thinking that, just on its own the letters that would need to go back and forth, to find out that my request was authentic. No none of that, when the time came I put in my written request on a normal prison document and it was signed off the very same day. Such is the power of God. So back to the security and the big fencing, we had set up a prayer ministry team of prayer warrior intercessors, which I was also a part of and the mandate for the team was to pray for all the things revolving around the mission. So a price was given for that big fence and the dogs, and we had no money in the pot to cover it. So as we prayed to God for the money to come from somewhere we all agreed that it was not what God wanted, he wanted us to trust in Him and an army of mighty angels. That we would for the fourteen days and night have 24/7 prayer cover and just four guards with radio links to the police to raise the alarm should anything happen, especially at night, two guards walking around the outside and two guards walking around the inside.

And looking after it all was a man coming out each day from prison. All I can tell you is that when God moves, don't get in the way. I guess you now want to know the outcome of the event, it was a massive success, the tent had no fencing no dogs no police patrols at night, just the entrances secured with ropes, no padlocks or chains. Just four guards and a team of 24/7 prayer warrior, at that time the police thought we were crazy because there were many active criminals around the whole area, but we had total faith in God, as we had followed His plan and not our own. The police told us that at that time they were dealing with at least three street robberies a day, in that area. After the event the police reported that for the fourteen days the tent was on Clapham Common, not one single crime of any description had been reported in the area and in a radius of approximately one mile around the tent, not even a fold up chair was taken, and not even any attempt to enter the tent when it was closed. Such is the power of God. And now you see why I believe that God has got a profound sense of hummer, a convict coming out of prison to oversee a one point five-million-pound project with only four guards, this must make you laugh, sit up and pay attention.

During my time through that year, God showed me much of what the kingdom of God is all about, healings of many descriptions, the grace of God and His overwhelming love for us all, even people like me. How churches and people from different backgrounds if they chose to can put their differences to one side and work closely together for a common good. How different churches approach God and interpret the word of God through the Holy Bible. How they very often get things wrong. How things at times can get very ugly, and how the love and greatness of God can shine through in so many different ways. I am going to give you my honest opinion and belief of who I believe God to be and how by following Jesus Christ of Nazareth, your whole life and the life of you family and friends can be transformed by your Spirit through the power of the Holy Spirit, forever and into eternity

We first need to understand the story; this book you are now reading is a small part of a story, I hope and pray that this book will throw up more questions than answers, likewise to follow Jesus brings up more and more challenges in our life through challenging questions. I believe wholeheartedly that the Holy Bible is Gods story for our lives, if you follow any other faith, or have no faith then I strongly believe you are missing out on the one thing that can transform your life. This book is not about converting you from what you now believe for your life and that of your family and friends, it is to show you how a boy's life that was stolen by abuse and rape, and the wrong story and the impregnation of the beast, then went on to destroy the boy's adult life. How the only person that could perform spiritual surgery and cut out that beast, just a little at a time and after many years and operations, that boy became the man he was born and intended to be now with the right pictures in the right story.

The story is God's story in my life, the healer is Jesus Christ who died on a cross, was wrongly accused, beaten, bled and abandoned, on that cross so that I can live the life that God intended for me through the power of His Holy Spirit. Amen!

I am now JUST a Disciple of Jesus, I am not a teacher, a healer, a prophet, pastor, reverend, or minister of any kind, I don't have any special powers or work any miracles. I do all I can to help people in as many ways as I can, and to help lift them up, stand by their side, to help them rebuild their lives so they too can be and have the life they were born to have, to help them get into the right story for them and to live my life like Jesus, through reading and applying the word of God in my life. Don't forget I was shot at five times, at almost point-blank range, by a professional marksman and I should have been dead. If by what you read in this or other books that will follow, or through getting to know me or speaking with me, you think you would like to know Jesus, then I can point you in the right direction. You might already have Jesus in your life, but are you letting him lead your life? Then I can help you with that too. I can hear you saying "how?" Let's go on some more.

***

Life should be about constant change, because only through change can you grow, and there are many forms of change you can apply to your life. The one thing that we all have the same is that there is only twenty-four hours in a day, but it is very important how you use that twenty-four hours. If you are not prepared to make necessary changes then it is probably because of fear, you see life is mostly fought in a spiritual realm. If you believe there is a God then there has to be a devil, if there is day then there has to be night, the spiritual realm is scary and exciting and is the only way the devil can interfere in our lives. The devil only has one trick and objective for our lives, that is SEPARATION. But he has thousands of ways to achieve it. He wants to firstly separate you from God with lies, he wants to cause rifts in family life to separate you from the people you love. He wants to cause mayhem in your social life to separate you from your friends and much more. So, we need to guard our hearts because who we think we are on the inside makes us behave in certain ways on the outside how we hear things, how we see thing and how we say things.

If in life we get the picture wrong then the story will be wrong, and the outcome may not be to anyone's benefit. When I was ten years old to the age of sixteen, the picture in my life was wrong and as I was continually abused and raped, my heart was destroyed. I was impregnated with the seed of a beast, what I felt and saw in my life gave me the wrong picture and changed my story, it affected what I said and how I behaved. I was not a nice person, I was not the person God intended me to be, because of the people who raped me the devil was able to separate me from God, so as a consequence as I developed it was without any good influence in my life, and I became a loner and I could be very nasty. This is part of the devil's plan to distort the truth, to make right wrong and wrong right, at this time when I was living in my story it made massive changes to how I behaved and how I was perceived by others. I became a master at manipulation, disguise, and lies. Are you in the wrong story? Do you need to change your story? Perhaps you're in the right story but with the wrong picture.

Conclusion

I want to help you get the real story, the story that is meant for your life and mine.

In the beginning God created the heavens and the earth. The earth was without form, and void; and darkness was on the face of the deep. And the Spirit of God was hovering over the face of the waters.

Then God said, "Let there be light"; and there was light. And God saw the light that it was good; and God divided the light from the darkness. God called the light day, and the darkness He called night. So, the evening and the morning were the first day.

OK, don't panic I am not going to re-write the Bible, but the point I want you to understand is that, this is the right story, this is the story we are all meant to apply to our lives, and it is not meant to be done on our own. When I made the decision to be a follower and disciple of Jesus it transformed my life, remember I was in an old Victorian prison, and I had to find out why I was shot but didn't die? I had to have a healer, I was battered and bruised beyond recognition, I was numb and lifeless, I was smelly, dirty and in a dark miserable place. I didn't care if I lived or died, and I had been infected and impregnated with a beast, I had completely lost not just my story but any story, I didn't have a story. Then Jesus Christ, the risen son of God, the Nazarene, picked me up and told me He loved me! And that He would heal my wounds, wash me clean, forgive me of every sin, and I mean every sin and show me the life I was always intended to live.

Over the next seven years Jesus stood side by side with me through every day in prison, He never left me and to this day has never left me, He took me right back to the day I was conceived and healed every wound I had sustained, cast out the devil and the beast from my life, performed spiritual surgery on many occasions and by the time I was let loose back into society, I was now in the story I was always intended to be in.

Are you ready to accept Jesus as your saviour? To walk side by side with Him and let Him lead you in the right story, the story that was intended for you, are you ready for the most amazing spiritual surgery?

You may be of another faith; can I ask you one question? Were you born into that faith, and never been able or allowed to choose or look to see if you are in the correct story for your life and the life of your family?

Are you of no faith or have been damaged or put off Christianity by so called Christians through their interpretation and legalism of the Holy Bible?

Or are you like me, have you been raped and abused so badly you could never accept that there is even a God at all?

Come and walk with me, let me and others come alongside you.

Would you like the opportunity to be in the right story, to see the truth for your life and to have all the damage in the story you are in now put right, to be healed of the lies and cast out the infection that come from them?

Spiritual surgery occurs when you allow the Holy Spirit of God to make deep cuts into our innermost beings, exposing us for who we are (Hebrews 4:12-13). So what are the areas of your life that you need surgery for?

These are some of mine:

- My inner thoughts – Jesus search my innermost thoughts and help me to stay in the right story.

- My emotions – Jesus help me to keep control of my emotions, so I can stay in the right story.
- My prejudices – Jesus help me to evict all prejudices from my life, so I can be effective to help people in my story.
- My habits – Jesus help me to develop good practices that are in keeping with my story.
- My motives – Jesus help me to have the correct motives in helping people in my story.
- My attitudes – Jesus help me to have a positive attitude in my story.
- My addictions – Jesus help me to steer clear of making anything an addiction. So, I can clearly stay in my story.
- My hidden sins – Jesus cleanse me in my soul and spirit of any sin. And make me clean before you in my story.

Spiritual surgery is done on us by the Spirit of God using the Word of God as his scalpel, and this is known as the Sword of the Spirit. (Ephesians 6:17)

So now you are ready to accept Jesus the Son of God as your saviour, I would like to lead you through a short prayer and then give you information to help you connect with us.

Prayer.

Father God, the creator of all creation
and the most High God.
Listen to my prayer, the person who is reading
this book and responding to your call right now,
Spiritually take them into your arms and guide
them and accept them in the condition they are
in right now to lead them into union with your son Jesus
that through Him they can be resurrected in Him to have
union and fellowship with you to be in the right story
for their lives and have eternal life with you our
Most High God.
Amen.

Dear New Believer,

Greetings to you in Jesus' Name,

I am so happy to hear of your decision to accept Jesus Christ as your personal saviour, and to have Him lead you into the right story for your life. It would be great if you could say the following words as an act of faith in your life.

> *"Jesus Christ, I believe you can and will put me in the right story that has always been intended for my life, I ask you now to come into my life and I fully accept you as my Lord and Saviour. Amen"*

On the next page there is a Decision Card, it would be great if you could fill in your details, and forward it to us, as we know now you will have many questions and we would love to help you grow in your new story, the one you were always meant to be in.

Decision Card. (please print clearly)

Date.........................

Now that you are committed to Jesus Christ you are saved.

Name..

Male Female Adult (over 18 years) Youth (under 18 years)

Address..

....

Town...........................City..................................

Post Code.........................Country...........................

Email..

Phone...

Is this the first time you have decided to follow Jesus? Yes/No

If you submit your details to us we will get back to you within two weeks of receiving your acknowledgment, or you can respond on our website. (Not yet live).

Please email responses to fredpoole762@gmail.com

Don't just aspire to make a living, to just get by, aspire to make a difference as you are lifted up, put your hand behind you reach out to someone and bring them with you!